# The Shadow's Gift:

Who

*Beyond the veil of consciousness lurks your shadow side.*
*Learn how to engage it and become a whole person.*

# THE
# SHADOW'S GIFT

## FIND OUT
## WHO
## YOU REALLY ARE

ROBIN ROBERTSON, PH.D.

NICOLAS-HAYS, INC.
Lake Worth, FL

Published in 2011 by Nicolas-Hays, Inc.
P. O. Box 540206
Lake Worth, FL 33454-0206
*www.ibispress.net*

Distributed to the trade by
Red Wheel/Weiser, LLC
65 Parker St. • Ste. 7
Newburyport, MA 01950
*www.redwheelweiser.com*

First published in 1997 by A.R.E. Press
This second revised and expanded edition, published by Nicolas-Hays, Inc.

ISBN 978-0-89254-164-5

Library of Congress Cataloging-in-Publication Data

Book design and production by Studio 31.
*www.studio31.com*

Printed in the United States of America

# DEDICATION

For all my students at the California Institute of Integral Studies,
who have found that learning about the Shadow has
explained so much in their lives.

# Illustration Credits

*Dore's Spot Illustrations*, selected by Carol Belanger Grafton, New York: Dover Pictorial Archive Series, Dover Publications, 1987, figures 8, 13, 14, 15, 19.

*Encyclopedia of Witchcraft & Magic, The*, ed. Venetia Newall, New York: Dial Press, 1974, figure. 6.

*Hand Shadows to be Thrown Upon the Wall*, by Henry, Bursill, New York: Dover Publications, 1967/1859, figure 12.

*Humorous Victorian Spot Illustrations*, ed. Carol Belanger Grafton, New York: Dover Pictorial Archive Series, Dover Publications, 1985, figures 7, 10.

*Men: A Pictorial Archive from Nineteenth -Century Sources*, selected by Jim Harter, New York: Dover Pictorial Archive Series, Dover Publications, 1980, figures 3, 4, 17, 16.

*1001 Spot Illustrations of the Lively Twenties*, ed. Carol Belanger Grafton, New York: Dover Pictorial Archive Series, Dover Publications, 1986, figures 1, 11.

*Pictorial Archive of Decorative Renaissance Woodcuts*, ed. Jost Amman, New York: Dover Pictorial Archive Series, Dover Publications, 1968, figure 2.

*Picture Book of Devils, Demons and Witchcraft*, eds. Ernst and Johanna Lehner, New York: Dover Pictorial Archive Series, Dover Publications, 1971, figure 9.

*Ready-to-Use Old-Fashioned Romantic Cuts*, ed. Carol Belanger Grafton, New York: Dover Pictorial Archive Series, Dover Publications, 1987, figures 5, 18.

# Table of Contents

*We develop body armor to protect is from life. We become rigid and unyielding. In order to make changes in life, we have to break down that rigidity and become flexible once more.*

# INTRODUCTION:
# ME AND MY SHADOW

as a boy I loved to kick a rock
half buried in the earth out
along the ground
and suck from the damp socket
the shadow
the stone's secret self. We come out
of the ground like this, rolling
as though searching, hoping
to find that fit again.

RICHARD MESSER.

Psychologist C. G. Jung once said that all change is experienced by the ego as a death. It's a long, slow process to develop into the person we are. Abraham Lincoln once remarked that he didn't like a man's face. When his companion criticized him, saying "he can't help his face," Lincoln answered calmly that "after a certain age, every man is responsible for his face." In other words, we are each responsible for our lives; the moral choices we make throughout the course of our lives are reflected in us so deeply that others can see them in our face, our voice, our walk, our every action.

Psychologist Wilhelm Reich's clinical studies confirmed Lincoln's astute observation. Reich found that our bodies are literal mirrors of our souls. Our muscles set in patterns which are indicative of the choices, good or bad, we have made in our lives. We develop body armor to protect us from life. We become rigid and unyielding. In order to make changes in life, we have to break down that rigidity and become flexible once more.[1]

9

The person we are is the product of many choices which we have made along the course of our life. We each begin with a unique set of possibilities determined by our inborn abilities and our outer circumstances. These provide the material with which we can paint the portrait of our life. However, it's the choices we make in life which actually paint the picture.

Over the course of our lives, each of us has taken paths that others haven't taken. We have each accepted certain ways of doing things because they fit us and denied other ways because they just were not us. Over time, those paths, those choices, have made us the person we are, and that person is less and less likely to change. When we are confronted by a new challenge, we are prone to fall back on solutions which have been hard-won in past struggles.

However, inevitably life presents us with problems which can't be solved with old answers. These are the problems that demand a change in our life. We know it, but resist knowing it. We force an old solution onto a current problem, pretending that, while it might not fit perfectly, it's close enough. Of course it isn't really. We're just applying the ostrich principle of sticking our heads in the sand and hoping the problem will go away. If, through fear or rigidity, we continue this behavior long enough, we begin to cause ourselves real suffering.

It seems too much to expect that we have to change still one time more; after all, haven't we changed so many times before? We feel unfairly treated by life. However, as Robert Green Ingalls said: "in nature there are neither rewards nor punishments—there are consequences." We aren't being singled out for punishment; we are merely experiencing the consequences of our own rigidity. If we choose security over change, we have to suffer the consequences. As Gail Sheehy summarizes succinctly: "If we don't change, we don't grow. If we don't grow, we are not really living. Growth demands a temporary surrender of security."[2]

We can learn how to recognize our own rigidity and how to correct it. It takes honesty and courage, but the rewards are immense. First, the suffering stops. This is the surest sign that we have chosen the right path again: the unnecessary suffering stops. More importantly, new possibilities open up everywhere in our life. Where everything seemed sterile and barren and there seemed no possible answers, now everything seems possible. The possibilities may be scary, because each offers a path that we have never taken before, but it's a good kind of fear, like the fear that a fine pianist experiences before a concert.

GED'S STORY:
HELLO DARKNESS MY OLD FRIEND

*[Jung] told me that he once met a distinguished man, a Quaker, who could not imagine that he had ever done anything wrong in his life. "And do you know what happened to his children?" Jung asked. "The son became a thief, and the daughter a prostitute. Because the father would not take on his shadow, his share in the imperfection of human nature, his children were compelled to live out the dark side which he had ignored."*

A. I. Allenby
describing a conversation with C. G. Jung.[3]

There is nothing so frightening as facing the darkness within—our inner shadow. We will do almost anything to avoid having to look into the dark places of our soul. And rightly so. The darkness contains much that we mere humans can't face. There is evil, of course; we're all too familiar with that, but there is also much more that is neither good nor bad, but merely beyond our human capacity to comprehend. Wonder and beauty and all our future possibilities also lie hidden in the darkness, and far too often in our shortsightedness, we confuse them with evil. When we start to automatically dismiss something as evil when in fact it is merely outside our normal experience, we should remember the words of poet/painter/religious mystic William Blake: "Everything possible to be believed is an image of truth."[4]

There is no change that doesn't begin in the darkness of the human soul. We first have to discover an entrance into the darkness, then we have to light a tiny candle in the dark so that we can search for our future self, and finally we have to join with it. And that takes resourcefulness, and patience, and most of all courage.

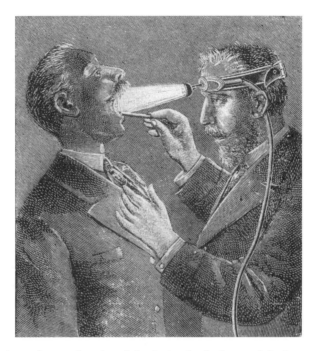

*There is no change that doesn't begin in the darkness of the human soul. We first have to discover an entrance into the darkness, then we have to light a tiny candle in the dark so that we can search for our future self.*

The necessity for the confrontation with the shadow has been known by all cultures in all times and recorded in their myths and legends. I'm fond of a modern fictional version by science fiction writer Ursula Le Guin. In *A Wizard of Earthsea*[5], she tells the story of a world where magic still rules and wizards go through years of training at an academy, much as doctors or lawyers might today. One young wizard-in-training, Ged, already realizes that he has powerful magical abilities, which he is chafing at the bit to use. Challenged by another student to demonstrate that power, he determines to raise a spirit from the dead, the spirit of a very great lady who died over a thousand years before. Ged's power is great enough that he succeeds at his task, but in the process a shadowy creature also emerges, a creature of darkness and evil, a creature with no name. Ged has no idea what it is, though something about it is vaguely familiar.

The shadow nearly kills him before Ged is saved by the Archmage Nemmerle, the head of the academy and its greatest wizard. But though he forces the shadow to flee, even Nemmerle cannot return the darkness to its home. The effort is so great that Nemmerle dies afterwards. Though Ged has survived, his face is deeply scarred, and the shadow is loose in the world, looking for an opportunity to finish what it started with Ged. There is seemingly no way to conquer the shadow because no one knows what it really is or what its true name might be.

> As we will see later, this is one classic way to release the shadow: through our hubris and arrogance. And at this early stage, we have no idea who or what has been released, and certainly don't associate it with ourselves. Though, like Ged, we may find it "vaguely familiar."[6]

For a long time, Ged wishes for death, sure that he has forfeited his future for the sake of a moment's prideful indulgence. Slowly he resumes his training as a wizard, since there is little else available for him. At least, as long as he remains at the academy, he is protected from the evil he has loosed in the world. Eventually though, he completes his training and goes out into the world, constantly on guard since he never knows when he might once again be attacked.

> At least the appearance of the shadow tends to cure us of hubris, and forces us to engage more consciously with the process of our own development. This is a period when one just has to put one foot in front of the other and keep moving, with no idea where the path might lead.

Ged accepts a position as wizard for a small fishing village which has the rare bad luck to be threatened by nearby dragons. While he remains there largely as security against dragons, he also performs the many small chores that a wizard can do for such a community. Though respected by the villagers, he remains a lonely, isolated figure.

> The path of inner development is inevitably a lonely one, because there are no outer solutions to our problem. And very few ever follow such a path.

Somehow he does become friendly with one of the villagers, but even that causes him further grief when his friend's small boy becomes desperately ill. While trying to cure him, Ged realizes that the boy is already dying. In desperation, he sends his spirit forth after the spirit of the boy, into the dark place that lies between the living and the dead. And there he once more encounters the shadowy creature of darkness. Somehow Ged manages to fight it off and return to the human world, where he again lies as if dead for days. The boy is dead, Ged has once more nearly died, and his fear of the shadow is now almost crippling.

> The difference here from his first encounter with the shadow is that it comes not from his arrogance and hubris, but from his compassion for another. This time Ged has taken a first step into the nether land that lies between normal consciousness and the world of the shadow. But he is ill-prepared and nearly perishes. Thankfully, few encounters with the shadow have to be so dramatic.

When he recovers, he realizes he is a danger to the villagers as long as he remains with them. Yet he cannot leave without abandoning them to the threat of the dragons. So he determines that he must face the dragons. If he survives, which he doubts, he will then leave. At least if he dies, it won't be due to the shadow.

> Up to now, Ged's life after releasing the shadow has been without purpose. He has merely been filling in time waiting for an encounter that might come at any time or at no time. Now, for the first time, he is consciously engaged with a quest; he is trying to achieve a goal which is greater than himself and his personal survival. This is the first great leap-of-faith that we all have to take: the acknowledg-

ment that there is something more important than our own petty concerns.

Ged goes to the island where the dragons live. Attacked, he slays five small dragons—if such a concept as small can be applied to dragons. Then he comes to face the great dragon who is mother of all the dragons on the island. Dragons are wise, but think and speak in ways that are strange to humans, so Ged has to learn to read the meaning that lies beneath her outer words. She thinks Ged has come to steal her treasure, but Ged insists that he only wants safety for the villagers. The dragon reveals that she knows of the shadow who pursues Ged and perhaps can give him its true name. This disturbs him, as it didn't seem possible that the shadow could have a name. When Ged resists even that temptation, the dragon decides she is tired of negotiating and will simply kill Ged. But Ged has been smart enough during their discussion to deduce the dragon's name. With that name and his wizardry, he has power over the dragon. The dragon is forced to agree that none of the dragons will ever harm the villagers again.

> This marks the stage where we successfully face great trial, and win through to a deeper level of knowledge that seems inhuman and amoral. One of the hardest tasks in facing the shadow within us is that the nice, clear-cut black-and-white moral values we have lived with so long are revealed to be inadequate to deal with the difficulties we encounter. Instead we come to face a deeper level of knowledge and morality which doesn't fit comfortably into human categories.

Ged can now leave the villagers in safety and proceed on his lonely way. He has further adventures, each of which increases his powers. Each adventure also brings a further encounter with the shadow, which increases his fear. Eventually there comes a time when he realizes that he can no longer remain the hunted, but must become the hunter. Instead of fleeing from the shadow, he turns and tries to seek the shadow. Though he has no conscious knowledge of where the shadow might be, something in him provides the path.

Each time he approaches the shadowy figure now, it is the shadow who flees, reduced to setting traps for Ged in his wake. But Ged continues to pursue the shadow past the ends of the earth, to seas where no one has ever sailed.

> As long as we run from the shadow, denying any relationship with us, we have no chance of finding the treasures it has to give us. Hopefully reading this book will help the reader to turn and face their own shadow without having to follow quite so circuitous a path as Ged does. But regardless of when and how we face the shadow, it will always be "past the ends of the earth," on "seas where no one has ever sailed." This is because the shadow problem demands a unique solution from each of us.

Eventually there comes a time when there is nowhere further to flee and the time of confrontation arrives. The shadow takes on many forms as it tries to subdue or elude Ged, but Ged stands fast, holding forth a wizard's staff glowing with light. The final moment arrives when Ged speaks the shadow's name, and the name is Ged!

> Ged reached out his hands, dropping his staff, and took hold of his shadow, of the black self that reached out to him. Light and darkness met, and joined, and were one.[7]

Having done so, Ged was once more whole and well and began his true journey, which would make him the greatest wizard of all.

> All the wonders and mysteries of the shadow are finally revealed. When we finally realize that we are the shadow, and the shadow is us, we become incredibly expanded. There is a beautiful passage in the Bible that fits this revelation: "When I was a child, I spake as a child, I understood as a child, I thought as a child: but when I became a man, I put away childish things."[8]

This book is about the shadow contained in each of us, and why, like Ged, we must each join with our shadow in order to become whole. In our study of the shadow, we will be drawing heavily on the work of famed depth-psychologist C. G. Jung, but the reader need not fear that this will be too technical. We are talking about things that concern each and every one of us. If occasionally we have to use a psychological term, you can be sure that we will bring it down to earth and show just what it means in our lives. Along the way, we will come to understand each part of not only Ged's story, but of many other shadow stories as well: stories from real people's lives, from the Bible, in fairy tales or legends, or from modern fiction. No matter what form the protagonists might take, all are ultimately heroes, since there is no way to confront the shadow without becoming a hero in the process.

*The only way to discover the new personality hidden within us is to hold the tension of opposites long enough that something new emerges which is neither our current position nor the shadow position.*

# CHAPTER I

# The Call from Within:
# Why The Shadow Appears

In the hand of Pandora had been placed by the immortals a casket or vase which she was forbidden to open. Overcome by an unaccountable curiosity to know what this vessel contained, she one day lifted the cover and looked in. Forthwith there escaped a multitude of plagues for hapless man—gout, rheumatism, and colic for the body; envy, spite, and revenge for his mind—and scattered themselves far and wide. Pandora hastened to replace the lid; but one thing only remained in the casket, and that was *hope*.

CHARLES MILLS GAYLEY.[9]

The early part of our lives is spent trying to discover who we are with respect to the world outside us. While we're still children, the world can be a pretty scary place. It's more important to us to be safe than to be unique, and we're happy to have a family that protects us. When we become young adults, the world may still seem frightening, but it can also be very alluring. We leave our parents behind, take a few risks, and, in the process of taking those risks, start to discover who we are. We may take a few knocks in the process, but gradually we grow more sure of ourselves, more confident of who we are and where we are going.

Just then—when we're on top of the world, flush with success—the shadow appears! It always appears when it is least expected. Whenever we begin to think that we're pretty special, that life is going to get better and better, darkness shatters our complacency.

That's because defining who we are solely in terms of the outer world produces a shallow person, almost literally two-dimensional, with a face we present to the world, but no depth behind it. Imagine a flat paper doll—everywhere we turn we present the same face to the world. When we look in the mirror, that's still basically the face that we see, though we may pretty it up a bit in our mind to avoid having to see the blemishes that others see. No one, not even yourself, sees the face that's hidden on the other side.

Before the shadow appears, we are likely to think of our self almost exclusively in terms of our work role—architect, psychologist, secretary, politician—and our family role—mother, father, husband, wife. The trouble with such self-definitions is that since they are defined not by us, but by our place in the world, they fit anybody. Calling our self an architect doesn't tell us much about who we really are. Maybe we think of our self as a good architect or a creative architect, but there is nothing there that is unique to our own individuality. This is even more true in terms of our family roles. "Mother," for example, is so all-encompassing a role that there is precious little room left for the individual. Because so much of our life is spent in one or another of these roles, we forget that we are more than those definitions imposed on us from without.

Something deep inside us knows that we possess a unique identity, and it's not the face we present to the world nor is it the image that we pretend to see in the mirror. Instead this unique identity is a work-in-progress, a goal we are trying to achieve, a destiny that we come closer to or drift further away from as we grow and develop. In the course of our development, we learn how to set conscious goals that we can hold in front of our eyes like a carrot in front of a donkey. But when it comes to achieving unconscious goals, we hardly know where to start. We need to remember that "character, like a photograph, develops in darkness."[10] But then how can we follow our destiny when we don't know what it is, when it's hidden in darkness?

It would be nice if we were wise enough to tell ourself: "I've gone as far as I can go with the outer world, now it's time to look inside and see who I really am." But nobody is wise enough to do this—nobody! After all, we've worked long and hard to develop a comfortable self-definition, one that those around us are comfortable with, which makes us comfortable in turn. It would seem idiotic to try and redefine ourselves just when we think we know who we are. So instead we have to be dragged into change, kicking and screaming all the way.

But as we are resisting with all our strength, we need to remember that the shadow is a necessary part of our total personality. As long as it remains unconscious, we are incomplete. People differ widely in "their ability to stand such unwholeness. Some go through life oblivious of their one-sidedness, while others are more sensitive to the demands of the repressed factors without them."[11] But the shadow is always trying to force us toward wholeness. "When the obligation to become whole is laid upon an individual . . . . the first task he must undertake is to confront his shadow."[12]

## THE UNCONSCIOUS:
## WHAT LIES HIDDEN BEHIND
## THE BACK DOOR OF OUR PERSONALITY

*Consciousness is like a surface or a skin upon a vast unconscious area of unknown extent. We do not know how far the unconscious rules because we know nothing of it. You cannot say anything about a thing of which you know nothing.*

C. G. Jung.[13]

First a little background on the territory where the shadow lives. For most of us during the first half of our life, the world around us seems so large that we can't imagine we will ever find our place in it. We are so busy with that process that it never occurs to us that there might be a still bigger world inside us, but there is. Throughout this book, I will use the word *unconscious* to refer to this inner world, but that word is only used to indicate that there is a world of which we are not aware. You may also have heard it called the *subconscious*. The prefix *sub* indicates that this level of consciousness seems to be below or behind our normal consciousness; in no way should *sub* be taken to mean that the subconscious is inferior to normal consciousness. Some like to split the unconscious into a subconscious and a *superconscious*, stressing that the unconscious contains elements more primitive than normal consciousness and elements more advanced than normal consciousness. Though there is some truth to that view, we are better off not splitting the unconscious that way; far too often, we discover that the seemingly primitive and the seemingly divine are inextricably connected within the unconscious. It is our conscious attitude that splits them into categories; inside the unconscious they are merged.

Another way to split the unconscious is to divide it into a *personal unconscious* and a *collective unconscious*. The personal unconscious contains memories that we have gathered in our personal lives, which have either never become conscious or were once conscious and have now retreated below conscious awareness. In life, we find that there is no real clear-cut boundary between consciousness and the personal unconscious; memories, feelings, thoughts move vaguely between one and the other.[14] The collective unconscious seems to contain the entire history of not only our species, but of all life. It is so large that the personal unconscious is just a tiny speck within it, like a single planet compared with the universe. But, of course, the collective unconscious is further from normal consciousness and only emerges into consciousness with effort.

The collective unconscious isn't as mysterious as it sounds. All species evolved from earlier species over great lengths of times, and all contain the remnants of that evolution, both within their physical and neurological structures. Nineteenth century German biologist and philosopher Ernst Haeckel argued that, in the development from egg to birth, each individual of a species goes through the same stages as the evolutionary history of the species. He had a wonderfully descriptive catch-phrase for this: "ontogeny recapitulates phylogeny." As with so many useful descriptive models, the actual individual development (ontogeny) is more complex than this single phrase would have it. Still, nature doesn't throw away anything useful. When we look in the ocean depths, we find creatures little different from their ancestors of hundreds of millions of years ago; e.g., some that are little more than swimming tubes that absorb any food that passes through them on their unending journeys. Then, when we look inside land animals (including humans), we find alimentary canals that are almost identical in structure to these primitive animals. Nature found something useful and built a larger structure around it.

Similarly in the structure of the human brain, we find a series of three largely separated brains stacked upon each other, each appearing at a later point in time, each handling more specialized or more advanced needs. This *triune brain* model was originally developed by neuroscientist Paul D. MacLean in the 1960's and popularized by Carl Sagan as part of his best-selling book, *The Dragons of Eden.*[15] Neuroscience has continued to advance since this model was proposed, and, as with Haeckel, the actual evolution of the brain has proved more complex than MacLean's model. But the triune brain model can still help us understand why humans behave in ways that don't fit readily into our vision of ourselves as rational beings.

There is actually a fourth brain which is more ancient than any of the three brains: the *neural chassis* (to use MacLean's phrase for the spinal cord, hind- and mid-brain). It takes care of all the automatic functions of the body, including protecting ourselves and reproducing. Sagan says that "in a fish or an amphibian, it's almost all the brain that there is." He goes on to quote MacLean as saying that for any higher animal, if that was all that there was, they would be "as motionless and aimless as an idling vehicle without a driver."[16] The three brains of the triune brain are the drivers.

The most ancient of the three brains, the *reptile brain* (more properly the "r-complex"), first appeared approximately 250 million years ago in the age of dinosaurs (hence Sagan's striking title). The *mammal brain* (more properly the limbic system) arrived roughly 100 million years later. Finally, the *primate brain* (the neocortex) appeared barely tens of millions of years ago. It developed immensely as humans evolved several millions years ago, so that we can probably now refer to the neocortex as the *human brain*, provided we realize that it also contains within it the evolutionary history of our primate ancestors.

The reptile brain is located at the top of the brain stem which leads into the spinal cord. When the mammal brain evolved later, it simply wrapped around the reptile brain. And wrapped around it in turn is the neocortex, that almost infinitely wrinkled surface which we normally think of as the human brain. Though all three brains necessarily communicate to some extent, in large part they take care of their own business without interference from each other. That is the significant point for us: each brain is largely independent of the others! And often that results in our feeling split inside over issues.

For example, the reptile brain handles issues of aggression, territoriality, social hierarchies, and ritual. That's what is in control when we get "territorial" and "aggressive" because someone is flirting with our boy friend or girl friend, or someone has a bigger office than we do, or some scholar in our field publishes an idea we regard as our own. The mammal brain governs social issues and the more complex emotions that accompany them: "belonging, caring, empathy, compassion and group preservation."[17] It's a fascinating fact that these are the parts of our behavior that we consider most human, yet they are actually what we share with our cousins in the animal world. In contrast, the uniquely human brain is the developed neocortex, the reasoning, cognitive brain. It probably first appeared as human beings became upright and depended more and more on their sense of vision. For that reason, it could also be fairly termed the visual brain.

We might think of the stages when each of these three brains reigned supreme as stages of the development of consciousness, if we consider consciousness on a spectrum that fades down to that which is totally unconscious. The relative lengths of time since each developed corresponds roughly to the amount of control each has over our lives (though I'm stretching the point a bit here). Thus far and away the most vital regulator of human life is the neural chassis, which directs the autonomous functions of our body and of which normally we are totally unconscious. Then the reactions of the more primitive reptile brain (which is deeply involved with shadow issues) generate a great deal of our interaction with the world, and again these are largely unconscious. We might regard the mammal brain as the beginning of the simplest levels of consciousness, though at that point, we get into controversies about what consciousness is or is not.

Until fairly recently, both philosophers and scientists thought of the human brain as a *tabula rasa* (blank slate) on which our sensory experiences were recorded. As we can already see from our discussions of the triune brain (and I stress again that the actual evolutionary structure of the human brain is more complex than the model), nothing could be further from the truth. Instead we are born with an enormous amount of instinctual knowledge built into the very structure of the brain. Or perhaps more accurately the several "brains." Some of that stored knowledge is quite general, some surprisingly specific.

For example, the need for defense is so important that in many species, a baby is born instinctually knowing how to recognize its enemies. Famed naturalist Konrad Lorenz won the Nobel Prize for his observations of animal behavior which led to the new field of ethology. He commented that "A good many birds, such as magpies, mallards or robins, prepare at once for flight at their very first sight of a cat, a fox or even a squirrel. They behave in just the same way, whether reared by man or by their own parents."[18] In other species, such as jackdaws, evolution has instead chosen to have the parents pass on the knowledge of enemies to the children. Here the knowledge isn't inborn, but the need to pass on the knowledge by the parent is inborn; i.e., nature predisposes even lower animals toward cultural inheritance. And since birds are essentially flying reptiles, this inherited knowledge is necessarily stored in the reptile brain.

Though we think of humans largely learning only through such cultural inheritance, like all other animals, we possess an enormous reservoir of instinctual knowledge as well. Jung terms these stored patterns *archetypes* (from the Greek for *prime imprinter*). Jung chose to use the word archetype, instead of instinct, in order to emphasize that the same stored pattern might present itself through either instinctual behavior or through images. The simpler the creature, the more important instinct; the more complex, the more necessary that the pattern can be converted to an image which can be processed by the mind.[19]

And really the unconscious should not be considered as a place. We don't pick up memories from some storehouse, where they have been carefully placed and labeled. When we remember something, we are actually reconstructing a memory, in the process drawing on other related memories in our lives. When we perceive something for the first time, we are also drawing on related memories, so that when we think we are seeing and hearing something directly, we are really constructing that vision and that sound much like we do when we bring a memory to mind.[20] And obviously, that construction isn't under control of our consciousness, as it is going on all the time, waking or sleeping, without any effort or awareness on our part.

The unconscious can seem like a strange concept at first. As a first approximation, think of the unconscious as your whole being, both body and mind. The body is able to carry on virtually all its necessary functions with no need for conscious intervention. In fact, consciousness can get in the way; just make yourself aware of your breathing. You may find that your breathing becomes very irregular as your consciousness interferes with the normally unconscious process. Gradually your consciousness will turn to other matters, and you will find your breathing returns to normal.

Beyond that, a great number of our actions were once conscious, then became habits that no longer required conscious action. Again if we turn on our consciousness to these habits, we find it only gets in the way. As an example of this, try to make yourself conscious of everything that you do when you lie down to go to sleep. Unfortunately, this may lead to a sleepless night (or at least it will take a lot longer to go to sleep). Or pay conscious attention to your normal morning routine. Again you'll find that consciousness gets in the way.

As an example that approaches closer to the shadow, think of a time when you suddenly found yourself behaving inappropriately, perhaps bursting into anger that was out of proportion to the situation. At such times, your first thought is often "where did that come from?" Well, it came from the unconscious. Or think of the slips of the tongue that Freud so popularized that they are commonly called "Freudian slips". These slips tend to reveal actual feelings just beneath the surface of consciousness.

## A Psychic Seesaw: the Shadow as Balance

*The conscious mind is on top, the shadow underneath, and just as high always longs for low and hot for cold, so all consciousness, perhaps without being aware of it, seeks its unconscious opposite, lacking which it is doomed to stagnation, congestion, and ossification. Life is born only of the spark of opposites.*

C. G. Jung.[21]

Outwardly, we may be limited people with a limited identity; inside, we contain the universe. And it is an organized, purposeful universe. It seems to contain a template for our destiny in life, a template so detailed that it pictures who we should be at any point in our life and who we might become, a template that can adapt to the widely varying environments into which we are born, grow, and develop. When the person we are becomes too different from this template, the shadow appears!

As a first approximation, think of the shadow as an equal and opposite reaction to the face we present to the world. If we are outgoing and friendly, the shadow will be introverted and standoffish, and vice versa. If we like to solve problems by first gathering all the details and sorting them out, the shadow will instead prefer to ignore the details and see the big picture. If we prefer to deal with problems objectively, ignoring extraneous human issues, the shadow will concentrate on the emotional tone that underlies a problem and ignore the supposedly objective facts.

To the extent that we are able to include both sides of the above dichotomies within our behavior, the shadow is much the same as our conscious personality. So far this seems to be almost a mechanical process, much like a thermostat. But it is much more than that, since it seems to take account of that inner template of who we are intended to be. While the shadow compensates for what is lacking in our outer personality, it does so within the dimensions of what sort of person we are intended to be. During the first half of our life, while we each are developing in our particular way, we are not usually particularly bothered by the shadow when it appears to tell us we are out of line. It is only after we have achieved a self-definition that is successful in the world that the shadow appears to demand wholeness.

In *Modern Man in Search of a Soul,* Jung described that point in our life this way:

> The nearer we approach to the middle of life, and the better we have succeeded in entrenching ourselves in our personal stand-points and social positions, the more it appears as if we had dis-covered the right course and the right ideals and principles of behavior. For this reason we supposed them to be eternally valid, and make a virtue of changeably clinging to them.[22]

That is just when a *mid-life crisis* may appear and with it a shadow who does have to be taken very seriously. In the introduction to her best-selling book *Passages* author Gail Sheehy described how it hit her at the tender age of 35: "Some intruder shook me by the psyche and shouted: *Take Stock! Half your life has been spent. What about the part of you that wants a home and talks about a second child? Words, books, demonstrations, donations—is this enough? Suppose you died tomorrow? What of lasting value would you have contributed to the world?* To be confronted for the first time with the arithmetic of life was unnerving."[23]

The shadow that appears in our life at such a point doesn't just take a position equal and opposite to our outer personality, it takes a counterbalancing position around a center that portrays the person we are intended to be. This is all very mysterious. It seems best to accept that we contain within us access to a higher power which demands that we make our best effort to fulfil our unique destiny. How we interpret that higher power doesn't seem to be impor-tant. The important fact is that we have a gateway to something more than human within us. And though each of our destinies are unique, in all cases, the unconscious pushes us toward wholeness. Not toward perfection, toward wholeness!

## VIRTUES AND VICES:
## TOO MUCH OF A GOOD THING CAN BE DANGEROUS

*We must begin by overcoming our virtuousness, with the justifi-
able fear of falling into vice on the other side. This danger certainly exists, for the greatest virtuousness is always compensated
inwardly by a strong tendency to vice, and how many vicious
characters treasure inside themselves sugary virtues and a moral
megalomania.*

C. G. Jung.[24]

It would seem that striving to improve ourselves could never be
anything but good, but life isn't that simple. The more we seek the
light, the more darkness forms in compensation, in an attempt to
make us whole. The appearance of the shadow is in many ways a
sign that our picture of reality has become overly simplified, too
black-and-white, and needs more shadings of grey. Any virtue carried too far can become a vice, and any vice, if persisted in long
enough, can lead to virtue. In William Blake's radical phrase: "The
road of excess leads to the palace of wisdom."[25] Because of this, our
breakthrough into the darkness often comes not from our virtues,
but our vices.

One such way to release the shadow is through arrogance, as in
Ursula Le Guin's story of Ged. You'll recall that when he was dared
to demonstrate his hidden powers, rather than admit that he wasn't
ready, he went ahead and pretended to an expertise beyond his grasp.
And that act released his shadow, much as Pandora's insatiable curiosity caused her to release pain and misery into the world when she
opened her famous box. Like Pandora's box, once released, there is
no way to put darkness back into the box. It doesn't matter whether
we release it through curiosity or arrogance or vanity or jealousy or
avarice or any other quality, positive or negative. Once darkness is
loose, there is no putting it back again. But we also have to remember that one thing still remained in Pandora's box after evil was
released into the world: hope! No matter how terrible it feels once
the shadow enters our life, it is ultimately a positive step toward
broadened future possibilities in our lives; we must never despair.

As an example, let me tell you how my own confrontation with the shadow began. In my mid-thirties I was happily married, a vice president of an important firm, a man on his way up. I was smug and self-satisfied, convinced that my life would go from triumph to triumph. I pictured myself as a Renaissance man, able to achieve success in the "bottom-line" world of business, able to solve the complex intellectual problems presented by data processing, yet also a person of taste and refinement, who appreciated books and music and art. I really thought I was something. Hubris comes just before the fall.

My philosophy, such as it was, could be summed up in a single phrase (as I had been fond of doing for a decade): There ARE relative values! That seemed very profound to me. By this I didn't imply only that all values are relative, that there are no absolutes. I also meant that relative values, human values, do have significance. They matter! Not a bad philosophy for a young man in his twenties, when I developed it, but hardly sufficient for the moral dilemmas which I was to encounter in my mid-thirties.

At the peak of my hubris, my best friend was fired: to me unfairly fired. A simple thing in the normal run of business; I had certainly fired enough people myself. Yet this was special because it involved my best friend. I couldn't reconcile the event with my view of how I thought life worked: life was supposed to be fair! I couldn't reconcile the unfairness of his firing with my moral convictions. Now when it was time for me to put my philosophy to the test ("there ARE relative values"), I found it painfully inadequate.

Without a moral base, I felt my entire reality tumbling around me. The one event was enough to destroy my painfully won sense of identity. From that point on, virtually every single thing I held stable in my life was taken from me one at a time. Amazingly, essentially every single thing also came back when I was reassembled. The person I became could have been recognized not only in the person I was before my long journey, but could have been seen in the young boy I once was. I have a picture of myself at four years old, and all the personality traits are already there. "The child is father of the man" as Wordsworth said so wisely. But first there had to be the long struggle with my shadow.[26]

## Uncomfortable Feelings:
## Sexuality Releases the Shadow

*The body is a most doubtful friend because it produces things we do not like; there are too many things about the body which cannot be mentioned. The body is very often the personification of this shadow of the ego. Sometimes it forms the skeleton in the cupboard, and everybody naturally wants to get rid of such a thing.*

C. G. Jung.[27]

One of the most common ways to release the shadow is through sexuality. Often in the process of defining ourselves within our family and our career, we put sex on the back burner, dismissing it as something only young people have to worry about. Before the shadow makes its appearance, we often think of ourselves as mature and beyond such thoughts, regardless of our chronological age. What we are really saying is that passion has gone out of our life, replaced by work and routine. And not necessarily just sexual passion.

Then suddenly we find ourselves bothered by sexual feelings that we thought we had put behind us. These are such uncomfortable feelings that we are likely to initially deny them out of hand. Though we continue to deny that we have any such sexual feelings, they don't go away; instead they intensify behind the scene. Often sexuality starts to crop up in our dreams. Even if we don't remember our dreams, we find ourselves waking with troublesome feelings, as if things had gone on that we really wouldn't like to think about. Eventually the dreams will push their way into our conscious awareness, even if we're the sort of person who thinks that "I never dream."

We might find ourselves getting irritated with people who are more sexually free than we are, and begin to see all sorts of undesirable traits in them that have nothing to do with sexuality. They simply seem like bad people to us.

There's a technical psychological term for this tendency to see our unconscious desires in others; it's called projection, and we'll talk more about it in chapter 4. Put simply, if we can't face up to unwanted desires or traits within ourselves, we project them out onto others.

There has to be some similarity between the traits we want to deny and the behavior of the person in question. Marie-Louise von Franz says that "seldom, if ever, is nothing of what is projected present in the object. Jung speaks therefore of a 'hook' in the object on which one hangs a projection as one hangs a coat on a coat hook."[28] But it doesn't take very much to get on our enemies list at such a time. Just seeing people flirting the way normal men and women flirt might be enough to set us off. We might dismiss them as silly, frivolous people who don't realize that life is a serious business. Depending on our personal morality, we may even decide that they are sinners on their way to hell. The important thing to realize is that we're seeing a hidden part of our own personality, not what is actually happening. Our projections provide a view into areas of our personality normally hidden from us. We might be shocked to discover what an objective observer would make of the same situation that seems so distasteful to us. But, of course, as such times, we are in no mind to listen to an objective observer.

The shadow is not necessarily trying to make us act on these denied sexual feelings; it's merely trying to get us to acknowledge them. Life energy is trying to make its way out of the unconscious. Because our bodies are very primitive in their abilities to classify energy, it is often experienced as sexual energy, since that's one of the few forms all of us have encountered. I remember when I had a gall bladder which was causing me so much pain that it had to be removed. Before the operation, I asked the doctor why I felt the pain in the pit of my stomach, when the gall bladder is located nowhere near the stomach. He explained that the inside of the body is so primitive neurologically that virtually all the nerve endings coalesce near the stomach. That means that we experience pain as being located in our stomach regardless of where it is located internally. Similarly we tend to equate these strange new feelings emerging from the unconscious as sexuality. One of the lessons that the shadow can teach us is that things are not always as we experience them.

*We tend to equate these strange new feelings emerging from the unconscious as sexuality. One of the lessons that the shadow can teach us is that things are not always as we experience them.*

I once had a patient, we'll call him Barry, who came to me deeply depressed. He had experienced a need for passion in his life, and confused it with a need for sexuality. He was still a young man in his early 30s, but he felt trapped with a wife and a child and a job that seemed boring. So he had several sexual affairs to relieve the boredom. When he entered therapy, his wife had left to stay with her folks, and he was on probation at work. As we worked together, the first thing we discovered was that he had once painted, but had given that up as childlike. He was outgoing and affable and, like many such, had drifted into sales. He loved that work, but as passion went out of his life in other areas, he lost that passion, too, and couldn't sell either. The shadow emerged to remind him that you can't live a life out of duty, you need passion.

He was shocked that I didn't find him morally reprehensible, but just kept looking for what was calling him. Over the course of a relatively brief time in therapy, he eagerly tried painting again and responded enthusiastically to various psychological exercises I gave him to try on his own. He was open to almost anything new. As his zest for life came back, he found that nothing new was needed in his life except reawakening the passion. He still loved his wife and child, he still loved sales, and painting turned out to be something that really wasn't as central as it might have seemed. At the end he went away a totally transformed man, with every single outward part of his life unchanged from before his depression.

## ENANTIODROMIA: A PERSONALITY FLIP-FLOP

*Every psychological extreme secretly contains its own opposite or stands in some intimate and essential relationship to it. Indeed it is from this tension that it derives its peculiar dynamism. There is no hallowed custom that cannot on occasion turn into its opposite, and the more extreme a position is, the more easily may we expect an enantiodromia, a conversion of something into its opposite.*

C. G. Jung.[29]

We have already pointed out how the shadow may appear when we have become too virtuous, or perhaps it is better to say when our morality has become too black-and-white. There is a real danger in any belief system that asks us to reject the darkness and strive unceasingly for the light. The more we divide our moral world into such clear-cut opposites, the more we are totally sure what is right and what is wrong, the more the opposite value forms in the unconscious. If we try to invariably be nice to everybody, in the unconscious a figure forms who is totally selfish. If we try always to tell the truth, in the unconscious a con man forms who lies about everything.

The more we deny these opposing forces within our psyche, the stronger the shadow grows. If the denial is too extreme, instead of engaging with the shadow, we flip our moral position entirely and become our opposite. There is a fancy psychological term for this— *enantiodromia*—which means "transformation into its opposite." Just as every coin has two sides, every sinner contains a saint, every saint a sinner. In one of C.P. Snow's novels, he tells of a successful businessman who one day gives up everything and becomes a wandering beggar. Similarly Jung tells of a man he knew who was a pious churchwarden who, "from the age of forty onward, showed a growing and finally unbearable intolerance in things of morality and religion." He became little more than a dour "pillar of the church." This continued until suddenly, at age 55, he sat up in bed and told his wife: "Now at last I've got it! As a matter of fact, I'm just a plain rascal."[30] From then on he led a wastrel's life, throwing away his money on the proverbial wine, women and song. And probably enjoying himself immensely in the process.

Or remember Charles "Chuck" Colson. During his years as Nixon's infamous White House counsel, he kept a plaque on the wall that read: "when you have them by the balls, their hearts and minds will follow." Later, in prison for his part in the Watergate coverup, he suddenly was transformed into a born-again Christian who preached "love your neighbor" and "turn the other cheek." The trouble with these moral flip-flops is that nothing has really changed, despite the appearance that everything has changed.

Any extreme position, by its very nature, equally defines its opposite. We allow ourselves to transform into our opposite because we find the tension of engaging with both sides of a moral dilemma to be intolerable. Yet that is exactly what is demanded by the unconscious. The shadow doesn't appear in order to make us suddenly throw away all of our values; it appears so that we will open our eyes to the possibility that our current values are too restricted. The only way to discover the new personality hidden within us is to hold the tension of opposites long enough that something new emerges which is neither our current position nor the shadow position. If we refuse to entertain both sides of a moral dilemma and instead settle for one or the other side of the issue, the unconscious will react. And eventually it will react with an enantiodromia. As Jung says:

> The tendency to separate the opposites as much as possible and to strive for singleness of meaning is absolutely necessary for clarity of consciousness, since discrimination is of its essence. But when the separation is carried so far that the complementary opposite is lost sight of, and the blackness of the whiteness, the evil of the good, the depth of the heights, and so on, is no longer seen, the result is one-sidedness, which is then compensated from the unconscious without our help. The counterbalancing is even done against our will, which in consequence must become more and more fanatical until it brings about a catastrophic enantiodromia.[31]

Earlier, we mentioned that before the shadow appears, we are like a paper doll with a single face we present to the world. The shadow is what forms on the opposite side. An enantiodromia occurs when the paper doll flips so that the shadow side faces out, and the side that faces out is now in darkness. But if we engage ourselves with the shadow, to try to discover who it is and what it wants from us, eventually the paper doll fills out and becomes a fully three-dimensional person. That's why the shadow appears to begin with; we have reached a point in our life when we need more dimensions to our personality.

### EARLY SHADOW DREAMS

*The mayhem and violence in some dreams are more part of their
structure than content. As clumsy and slapstick as they appear, they
are actually the crucible in which something tender and subtle is
being born.*

Richard Grossinger.[32]

We all do dream: traditional dream research has demonstrated that
dreaming occurs during the sleep phases marked by rapid-eye-
movements; hence called REM-sleep. Regardless of whether we
remember our dreams in the morning, all of us dream about an hour
and a half in total each night, during those phases of REM-sleep.
There is more recent research that perhaps we dream almost continuously during the night, regardless of whether we are exhibiting
rapid-eye-movements.[33]

And it's not just humans who dream. In our discussion of the
triune brain, we didn't point out that virtually all mammals experience REM sleep and, hence, dreaming. Anyone with a pet dog or
cat has noticed their bodies moving during sleep as if they were
running. Bsirds also exhibit something like REM sleep. This especially interests us given that many scientists think that birds evolved
from dinosaurs. Let's speculate that perhaps dreaming appeared
first in the reptile brain at a very crude level, added more complex
emotional components with the appearance of the mammal brain,
and became symbolic when the neocortex evolved more fully.

When the shadow awakens us to our dreams, we find ourselves
in a world which has a totally different set of rules, rules that are
nonsensical to consciousness. When we wake and try to make sense
of our early shadow dreams, they seem totally irrational by the rules
of the conscious world we live in. Since dreaming began so early
in evolution, this is hardly surprising. We only gradually begin to
understand that dreams speak symbolically rather than rationally
because dreams appeared in evolution long before language did.

Remember how confused Alice was most of the time she spent
in Wonderland, where none of the normal rules of life applied. In
the beginning, after following the White Rabbit down the hole,

she finds herself in a long hall lined with doors everywhere, but all locked. She does find a key on a table, but the key is too tiny to open any of the doors. Finally, behind a curtain she finds a tiny door that the key will open, on the other side of which is a lovely garden. But she's much too large to go through the door. She spots a bottle labeled "Drink me;" when she drinks it, she shrinks until she's just the right size to go through the door. But she's left the key behind on the table and she's now too small it get it. She then finds a cake that says "Eat me." When she eats it, she becomes enormously large. Totally at a loss in this strange new world whose rules make no sense, she starts crying and, since she's now so large, her tears fill the bottom of the room. Just then she sees the White Rabbit come running past her again. She stops crying and tries to ask him for help but he runs on, dropping his gloves and his fan in his haste. Alice picks up both and tries to think her way logically through her situation. While that is happening, without her noticing it, she's shrinking again until she's much smaller than she ever was before. She realizes it's because she's holding the fan and drops it just before she shrinks away to nothing. Now, being this tiny, she's in danger of being drowned by tears she shed when she was huge. And this all happens in her first moments in Wonderland.

"Down the rabbit hole" has passed into the English language as a phrase for going on a great adventure. And indeed the appearance of the Shadow with its concomitant dreams leads us into the unconscious on a great adventure. There are for us, as for Alice, doors to be opened, and only one leads us where we need to go. Initially we can't find a way to open the right door and can become frustrated and tearful. But gradually we do learn the rules of the dream world. And there are some general rules about shadow dreams that can help us understand them a little better.

At the early stages of dealing with the shadow, ambiguous but negative figures often appear in our dreams. Vampires and werewolves are common, as they are half-human creatures of the night. At this stage we are so set in our ways that someone who represents values we deny has to be seen as something less than human. But remember that during the night, vampires and werewolves have more than human power and can only be destroyed with great dif-

*Vampires and werewolves are common, as they are half-human
creatures of the night. At this stage we are so set in our ways that
someone who represents values we deny has to be seen as something less
than human. But remember that during the night, vampires and
werewolves have more than human power and can only be
destroyed with great difficulty.*

ficulty. Similarly, these unwanted thoughts and feelings that are trying to come to the surface are very powerful, and we will have an increasingly harder time resisting them.

A perfect example from literature of how the shadow appears at this early stage is J. R. R. Tolkein's creation, Gollum, who appears in both *The Hobbit*[34] and *The Lord of the Rings*[35]. Gollum has so degenerated over time through his greedy, gloating possession of a magical ring of power and invisibility that he has become a repulsive, slimy creature no longer recognizable as the Hobbit that he was to begin with. In *The Hobbit*, the hero, Bilbo Baggins, tricks Gollum and steals away with the magical ring, which he keeps for a number of years. Similarly, it is possible to lie and cheat with the shadow and get away with it for a while. But not forever. Frodo, the hero of *The Lord of the Rings*, illustrates the proper way to deal with the shadow. When he first comes across Gollum, he finds him as disgusting as does everyone else. However, instead of cheating him, like Bilbo, or killing him, as Frodo's man-servant Samwise, argues for, Frodo treats him firmly but fairly. Though Gollum continually tries to either overpower or trick Frodo in order to regain the ring of power, he is unsuccessful. Because of Frodo's compassion and integrity, Gollum serves as a guide through the dark lands of Mordor. Without Gollum, Frodo would have been hopelessly lost.

In our space age, aliens from outer space are another common form that the shadow takes when it first appears. Outer space is separated from our normal conscious, earthbound life, much like the darkness where vampires and werewolves flourish. And these are unpleasant, inhuman aliens, not wonderful beings who have traveled trillions of miles just to help us. It's fascinating how in recent years, the positive aliens of the original UFO stories, popularized in movies like "Close Encounters of the 3rd Kind," have given way to nasty aliens who do terrible things to those they abduct. It seems likely that this change shows that shadow feelings are emerging widely across the population and expressing themselves through these negative encounters with aliens. Here is an example of an alien shadow dream:

> A spaceship is going to leave this planet soon. The hero and a friend find out that one of the other men there is really an alien, who they think intends to kill them, or at least to incapacitate them in some way. So they lure him off the ship and sneak back on the ship themselves. It takes off early while the alien is still on the planet.

Here the dreamer is using much the same technique as Bilbo did with Gollum, assuming he can sneak away from the shadow and leave it behind. But that method won't work in the long run with the shadow.

Here's another example of aliens. In this case, it's quite fascinating that the shadow, represented by the aliens, is clearly presented as bringing light—i.e., insight—that the dreamer can no longer avoid. That's as it always is, from the darkness comes the new light:

In the dream, the dreamer is being chased by aliens. He runs out onto a jetty near his home, but the aliens dive into the sea after him. They were swimming around under the jetty. Then they loomed up into the sky. He tried to hide between the large boulders that made up the jetty, but they pinned him down with an intensely bright spotlight. A voice came into his head, saying: "You cannot hide from the light."

The dreamer woke up in a panic to see the full moon flooding into his room, shining into his eyes, and his newly acquired pet garter snake staring at him from the window sill where it was resting, after having escaped from its cage.[36]

If we are resistant enough to the call from the unconscious, our dreams may bypass even the partial humanity of such figures and produce repulsive nonhuman figures: especially spiders and bugs of all sorts. For example, at a time when I was first beginning to do a good deal more writing and speaking, I once had the following shadow dream:

A radio announcer is sitting at a table, like a large kitchen table, doing his show. As a gimmick, he is having the biggest insect in the world on his show. This thing looked like a cross between an animal and an insect. It was on the table in front of the announcer, but if it were standing up, it would have been six feet tall. It had a large body like a beetle, but it really wasn't like any known insect. It was more alien than that. Because of this, it wasn't as repulsive as an actual insect that size would have been. It seemed like some unearthly creature. At one point, the insect must have gotten restless, because it quickly got off the table and moved off. The announcer couldn't do anything because he was on the air. I was in a room nearby, trying to nap. I noticed the insect move and noticed that the door to the building was open. I thought about getting up to close it, but decided "to hell with it."

In this dream, the shadow takes the form of an enormous, repulsive insect. The "announcer" represented the part of my personality which was beginning to "broadcast" my ideas to the wider world through writing and speaking. Notice that the announcer thought that he could safely examine the shadow characteristics, but instead he finds that the shadow is independent and moves off the table. By this time, even my conscious personality becomes aware of it, but is not sufficiently engaged yet to deal with it. So the shadow is allowed the freedom to go out into the world on its own. As you can imagine, I came to discover that I couldn't just bring up material from the shadow for "broadcasting" without fully engaging with it.

Animals are less common as shadow figures, as they tend to have other associations in the unconscious, but sometimes they appear if we have some especially bad association to a particular animal; e.g., a rat or a vicious dog. In later chapters, we will talk more about how the shadow appears in our dreams. The general rule is that as we begin to engage consciously with the shadow, it evolves in our dreams, gradually progressing from repulsive, semi-human creatures toward ever more human, ever more positive, forms. Jungian analyst Julius C. Travis discussed this progression in his paper "The Hierarchy of Symbols" where he told about a patient he called "Mr. Baker":

> He came for help because he was having the same repetitive dream four or five or six times a night: that an unknown beast was battering down his bedroom door. He would awaken violently in a sweat of terror, with the sound of splintering wood and wild breathing and beating in his ears.[37]

Here we have the shadow as a wild beast actually "battering down his bedroom door." And the same dream is occurring "four or five or six times a night"! Clearly the unconscious is going to get its point across whether Mr. Baker wants to acknowledge it or not. Happily, as he began to engage with the unconscious in therapy, gradually the images progressed from a wild beast to less threatening representations, such as animals or people who he knew. This progression indicated that he had begun to deal with issues presented by the shadow.

*If we are resistant enough to the call from the unconscious, our dreams
may bypass even the partial humanity of such figures and produce
repulsive nonhuman figures: especially spiders and bugs of all sorts.*

Here's an example from a different dreamer whose shadow progression has advanced slightly. The shadow is still threatening, but the man has learned how to deal with it—at least indirectly:

A man was cornered by a big dog and had to jump on top of his car. The dog wasn't mean; he just didn't know the man. The man was only stuck on top of the car for a few minutes before the dog's owner came and got the dog. The two men laughed and teased about it.

Here it is clear that the shadow characteristics represented by the dog are not really dangerous; the dog and the man just need to get to know each other better. Sound advice for any dealings with the shadow.

One final famous dream, which illustrates what can happen when the shadow is ignored, might be in order. The Book of Daniel in the Bible tells how Daniel was able to interpret several mysterious dreams of King Nebuchadnezzar of Babylonia. Each was a dream which warned of the consequences of the king's arrogance. This was the king's final dream:

> There was a magnificent tree that stretched toward the heavens, providing food and shelter for both the animals who lived beneath it, and the birds who dwelled in it. Then one day both a watcher and a holy one came down from heaven and decreed that the birds and the animals must leave the tree, and tree must be cut down and destroyed, leaving only the stump in the ground. "And let his portion be with the beasts of the field, till seven times pass over him."

Daniel was troubled, but told the king that the tree represented the king himself, who at his best provided nurture and shelter for his people. But unless he changed from his arrogant ways and once more was merciful to this people, he would be cut down and become like an animal. The king chose to ignore this advice, and everything Daniel prophesied did in fact come to pass. After suffering this indignity, he finally realized Daniel might be right, repented, and was restored to glory. A perfect example of how if we deny the existence of the animal within us, we become that animal.

# CHAPTER 2

# THE SHADOW KNOWS:
# POSSIBILITIES HIDDEN WITHIN THE SHADOW

As long as an individual does not function out of substance, as long as he or she does not demonstrate material weight but exists as a kind of flimsy, wispy, transparent, indefinite entity, there'll be no shadow. And shadow is what is attached to all that is evil and reprehensible—nobody wants to be associated with a shadow because it means carrying guilt. Yet the only way to avoid casting a real shadow is not to have any materiality....If one is going to have weight and substance and be definite, one will drag a shadow along at the same time.

EDWARD F. EDINGER.[38]

Often the shadow tries to make an entrance into our life, but we pay no attention to it until it's too late. Fairy tales are full of this motif. For example, *Grimm's Fairy Tales* contains the story of "The Frog King."[39] Once there was a beautiful princess who had everything that she could possibly desire. (To be honest, she was probably a spoiled brat). One day she was in the green woods that surrounded the castle where she lived, sitting at the edge of a deep, cold spring, playing with her favorite possession: a golden ball. She tossed it into the air, then caught it, over and over. Suddenly, the unforseen happened: a toss went awry and she missed the ball. It bounced into the spring and sank to the bottom. When she looked into the spring for her golden ball, it could no longer even be seen. She had no idea the spring was that deep. The princess burst into tears and began wailing.

Circles and spheres are time-honored symbols of wholeness. Every spot on their surface is identical to every other spot. They have no

45

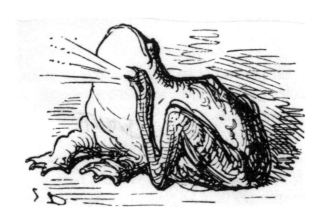

*The princess agreed with alacrity, thinking secretly
what a foolish frog it was to think he could be anybody's friend,
much less the friend of a princess.*

beginning or ending. Each contains the maximum amount within the minimum enclosure. And virtually all cultures have regarded gold as the most precious of the metals: beautiful and shiny, easily malleable, inert so that it never tarnishes. So the princess' golden ball symbolizes the precious wholeness of her previously blissfully unconscious life, now threatened.

Her cries were so piteous that a fat, ugly frog stuck its head out of the water and asked her what was the problem? When she told him that her ball had fallen into the water and she couldn't find it, the frog said he could get it for her. However, he first set a condition: he would only recover the golden ball if she would let him be her friend and constant companion, going with her everywhere.

This is a perfect description of how the shadow tries to make its way into our lives without causing us too much pain. When our lives are rosy and filled with material possessions, we tend to assume, like the spoiled princess, that we are so wonderful that we are entitled to everything good, and that nothing bad should ever happen to us. At that point, some magical thing goes out of our life, with its energy disappearing into the unconscious, just as the golden ball fell into the stream. That lost wholeness can only be recovered from the unconscious, and we need someone who lives there to help us. That is the shadow.

The princess agreed with alacrity, thinking secretly what a foolish frog it was to think he could be anybody's friend, much less the friend of a princess. Then the frog dove into the water and came up with her golden ball. The princess was so delighted that she immediately ran off with the ball, ignoring the poor frog who begged her to wait for him. After all, with his stubby little legs, he couldn't go fast enough to keep up with her. Unfortunately for the frog, now that the princess had her ball back, she no longer even remembered that she had agreed to let it be her friend and constant companion.

That's when the shadow appears, like the frog, helpful but ugly to our narrow vision. At such a time, we are willing to make any promises to get back what we have lost, but these promises are like New Year's resolutions, soon forgotten. Unfortunately, the shadow won't be ignored, when it appears again, it isn't always as friendly.


JOURNEY OF A DREAM ANIMAL: WORKING WITH YOUR DREAMS

*Dream images are so complex that we can never solve them; we can only engage with a shade of their partial solution, which becomes an image of a deeper riddle. Whether we partially decipher a dream or fail to decipher it, we change through our engagement.*

Richard Grossinger.[40]

It's important to form a habit of recording your dreams in a notebook or some other permanent form, so that you can go back and examine your dreams later. Often a dream will mean nothing to you when you have it originally and will only reveal its meaning over the course of time. But then understanding the meaning of a dream is not really the point of recording dreams. We record dreams in order to honor them; they are worthy of honor because all that we may ever become passes through our dreams before it is evidenced in our life.

The simple fact of making the effort to remember, then record your dream, opens a dialog with the unconscious. Once you begin consciously to react to the dreams produced by the unconscious, your conscious personality includes that awareness. Your unconscious then reacts in turn to this change. If you incorrectly interpret what the unconscious is saying to you, that wrong direction becomes part of you, and the unconscious usually makes it quite clear in future dreams that you've taken the wrong direction. Once the channel between conscious and unconscious is open, things proceed much faster. Jung stressed that the unconscious tends to respond to us in much the way we respond to the unconscious. If we dismiss our dreams as meaningless, we are unlikely to get much consideration from the unconscious; once we begin to acknowledge that our dreams might have meaning and purpose, the unconscious returns that respect and treats us with deference and compassion.

Though early shadow figures tend to be merely grotesque and frightening, they may already provide hints of what issues you are dismissing in your life. When someone first starts a Jungian analysis, they often have a "big dream" which shows the whole course of their future development. Similarly when you first begin to record your dreams, among all the dreams filled with inchoate, half-formed figures, you may find some which are already clearly defined and meaningful. For example, in her remarkable book *Journey of a Dream Animal*, Kathleen Jenks records this initial dream which led her on a long course of spiritual development:

> It was about a goldfish. It lay in a shallow container filled with mud and dirty water. I was repelled by the fish's reptilian flesh as it lay there, gasping for breath. But I could not let it die. I tried to push back the mud so that the fish would have a clear pool but the mud kept seeping back. Finally, in exasperation, I let him lie in the shallows. He would either have to die or revitalize himself without any outside help at all—and it was the one time when the little creature most needed that outside help! I went into another room for a while. At last, I went back to him and found he was still alive—more obviously so than before. I scooped away the mud and put him back in the water. As he lay in my hand, I could feel breaths sobbing in his gold flesh. I was terribly happy .... Anyway, somehow the creature got into a better fish tank and I was scheming to get a larger one for him when I awoke.[41]

Notice that Kathleen used the word "repelled" to describe the fish's "reptilian flesh," a sure sign that she's dealing with the shadow. Yet it's a "gold" fish; i.e., something clearly of value, much like the golden ball the princess loses in the story of "The Frog King." Kathleen comments that "the desperate little goldfish was my own spirit, but I did not realize that." Soon after in the dream, Kathleen begins "scheming to get a larger [fish tank]"; i.e., she begins to try and find a way to provide a better, larger home for her spirit, a way to honor the unconscious. In actuality, Kathleen, who was quite poor at the time, stole a book on Jungian psychology from the library and used the information in it to conduct a Jungian analysis independent of any analyst. Kathleen was able to use her dreams to advance her life past a desperate place in which she was stuck. One can hardly do better. And I think even the library might feel the book had found its rightful owner.

## THE "I" AND THE "NOT-I": WHAT'S A SOUL WORTH THESE DAYS?

*The distinction between what is "I" and what is "not-I" is not so easily made as most people assume.*

M. Esther Harding.[42]

Among the many stories about a man selling his soul to the devil is a medieval legend where, as usual, the man is offered wealth and power by the devil. When he asks suspiciously what he has to pay, the devil tells him slyly that all he has to give up is his shadow. This seems a small enough price to pay, so the man immediately agrees. "But then his troubles started, because nothing he did held any reality or substance." Seeing that he has no shadow, people are afraid that he is inhuman and begin to avoid him. Finding himself ostracized and lonely, he decides that he has made a bad bargain. He hunts for the devil, hoping he can persuade the devil to let him out of the deal. Unfortunately, no matter where he looks, he can never find the devil, for the devil "cast the man's shadow round him like a cloak and became invisible. He always stood just in the man's shadow."[43]

The above story is contained in *The "I" and the "Not-I"* by M. Esther Harding, who was one of the first psychologists to write about Jungian psychology for ordinary people. Her phrase "the 'I' and the 'not-I'" perfectly captures our relationship with the shadow. When the shadow first appears, it is precisely everything that we view as "not-I", all that has nothing whatsoever to do with our view of ourselves. But there's another way to look at it: "not-I" contains

*The greatest of all tales of selling one's soul to the devil is*
*Goethe's sort of Faust and Mephistopheles.*

everything there is except the minuscule amount of personality that
we have accumulated in our short life and think of as "I". "Not-I"
contains not only all the qualities we regard as bad, but also all the
qualities of people we admire, but think we have nothing in common with. The shadow serves the marvelous function of sorting out
for us just which of those unlimited number of qualities are those
we need, regardless of whether or not we think we need them.

Of course, since the shadow is immersed in the vast sea of
everything that is "not-I", it is only to be expected that at first it's
indiscriminate, mixing together everything dark and unknown hidden within, unable to separate what's needed from what's not. We
have to grapple with the shadow in order to get to know it, and until
we get to know it, we can't begin to sort out what parts belong to
our future and what parts need to be left behind in the darkness.

## Holding Tight:
### Jacob's Battle with the Mysterious Stranger

*And Jacob was left alone; and there wrestled a man with him until the breaking of the day. And when he saw that he prevailed not against him, and the hollow of Jacob's thigh was out of joint, as he wrestled with him. And he said, Let me go, for the day breaketh. And he said, I will not let thee go, except thou bless me. And he said unto him, What is they name? And he said Jacob. And he said, Thy name shall be called no more Jacob, but Israel: for as a prince hast thou power with God and with men, and hast prevailed. And Jacob asked him, and said, tell me, I pray thee, thy name. And he said, Wherefore is it that thou dost ask after my name? And he blessed him there. And Jacob called the name of the place Peniel: for I have seen God face to face, and my life is preserved.*

Genesis 33:24-30.

There is no way to avoid taking the time to engage with the shadow. This is perfectly illustrated by the Biblical story of Jacob's struggle in the dark with a mysterious stranger. Though the stranger struggled fiercely, Jacob had to hold him tight until daybreak, when he could ask for his blessing. The stranger then gave Jacob a new name: Israel—which means he who prevails with God. This little story already points to most of the key elements we need to remember in dealing with the shadow. Let's look at the details of the story and see what they can tell us about the shadow:

**Jacob had to wrestle in the dark with a mysterious stranger. Though the stranger struggled fiercely, Jacob had to hold him tight . . . .**

The battle with the shadow, like Jacob's with the mysterious stranger, is a fierce struggle, but one where our task is not to try to defeat the shadow, but merely to hold on. We will be constantly tempted either to deny the shadow's needs out-of-hand or to yield without struggle to its demands. If we do either, we lose the possibilities for change hidden within the shadow, that only a long struggle reveals.

## until daybreak . . . .

The struggle takes place inside the unconscious, and is only over when the light of consciousness fully reveals the shadow to us. Anyone who has ever gone through this struggle knows how difficult it is to struggle with values that are dark and murky. Far easier to walk along some nice well-lit path, to follow some outer set of rules that will tell us what is right and what is wrong. But once one begins the struggle with the shadow, no outer rules are ever sufficient again.

We have already discussed one important way to hold on to the shadow in the dark: dreamwork. There we stressed that the important thing is to record the dream and chew over it time and again. It's not so important to find its meaning—that would be the equivalent of beating the shadow—but since every dream has layer upon layer of meaning, there is no danger of exhausting it.

## . . . . when he could ask for his blessing.

We are asking for something from the shadow—his blessing—that's what the struggle is all about. At first the idea of being blessed by something that seems to represent every value we despise seems ludicrous. But after holding the shadow so close for so long, we grow intimate with it and its demands. At some point our acknowledgment of its legitimacy creates a bond in which the shadow not only blesses us, but we bless the shadow.

## The stranger then gave Jacob a new name: . . . .

If we stay the course, we will acquire a new identity, one that recognizes our accomplishment. This identity will be neither who we were before nor will it be that of the shadow (which happens when we yield too easily and an enantiodromia occurs). That new identity will be on a higher level from either and will partake of both our original identity and of the shadow qualities we needed.

Again we discover this in dreamwork. The series of shadow figures slowly evolve from nonhuman, to subhuman, to people we despise or fear, to people we tolerate but look down on, to casual friends, to close friends and family, until finally the shadow has become us. But, of course, we have changed in the process and acquired a new name and identity.

**Israel—which means he who prevails with God—"for as a prince hast thou power with God and with men, and hast prevailed."**

In struggling with the shadow, we are in some sense struggling with God, or at least with an intermediate force between humanity and divinity. Again it is almost unimaginable to us when we are first assaulted by the shadow, that it could in any way be associated with divinity. But it is. The shadow is our first experience of the "not-I" inside us. Ultimately we will find not only the shadow but many other figures, culminating in a numinous figure which Jung terms the Self. The Self is as close as we mere mortals can come to looking on the godhead.

We might also remember that Jacob was wounded in his thigh during the struggle. There is no way to prevail against the shadow without being wounded in the process. Often the wound is, like Jacob's, in the thigh, which is an oblique way of saying that the wound is to our sexuality. Just as often, the wound is to our emotional stability. Coming to acknowledge the shadow forces us to open ourselves to much inside our soul that previously we had denied. For men, that is most often feelings that had previously been so buried we didn't even know that they existed. In contrast, women often have to give up some of their sense of rootedness and connection to everything and everyone around them. The world after the shadow grows bigger than a sense of extended family can encompass. That is a growth, but also a wounding.

### PRIMITIVE (?) VS. CIVILIZED: TOO MUCH RATIONALITY ISN'T ALWAYS A GOOD THING

*But consciousness is equally relative, for it embraces not only consciousness as such, but a whole scale of intensities of consciousness.*

*Between "I do this" and "I am conscious of doing this" there is a*
*world of difference, amounting sometimes to outright contradic-*
*tion. Consequently there is a consciousness in which unconscious-*
*ness predominates, as well as a consciousness in which self-con-*
*sciousness predominates.*

C. G. Jung.[44]

The unconscious offers us possibilities that are simply not available to consciousness. In large part, this is because consciousness
has been too successful. In tribal cultures, the individual ego is still
largely subsumed within the collective ego; in other words, most of
a person's identity is supplied by tribal customs and values, which
have existed for generations upon generations. The individual only
rarely has to become conscious of him or herself as an individual,
with needs and values separate from the tribe. This doesn't mean
that the individual tribal members are interchangeable units like
ants in an ant colony; there is as much variation in personality and
ability in a tribe as in the supposedly more advanced Western cultures. But the one-sided directedness of consciousness is absent in
tribal cultures.

We consider ourselves rational beings because we use thinking instead of emotion. We consciously plan and act on our plans
instead of responding in the moment. Because of the power of
this stance, we forget the loss. Rationality is necessarily one-sided,
"even though the rational judgment may appear many-sided and
unprejudiced. The very rationality of the judgment may be the
worst prejudice, since we call reasonable what appears reasonable
to us."[45] Tribal members are still open to the unconscious; without
the defense mechanisms of individual ego consciousness, there is
still an open channel to the unconscious. Like a spirit medium or
a modern channel, the unconscious flows directly into the person
without conscious intervention, leading to immediate action.

In contrast, in so-called civilized men and women, our rationality necessarily excludes information from the unconscious. This
effectively cuts consciousness off from any new possibilities, possibilities that don't fit into our predefined definition of the "way
things are." Conscious and unconscious need to be joined in a con-

tinuous dance where the unconscious responds to the conscious position. To the extent that consciousness can in turn respond, the dance becomes lovely and intricate. To the extent that consciousness is cut off from the unconscious, each has to dance without their partner.

This isn't in any way to deny that consciousness wasn't the most important advance humanity ever took. As Jung said: "without consciousness, things go less well."[46] If rational ego consciousness cuts us off from the new information available from the unconscious, it also protects us from the continually shifting moods of the unconscious. We still experience these moods in collective settings like football games or political rallies. But the wonderful feeling of oneness we experience when we root for our team can easily lead to mob hatred of anyone who supports the other team. That feeling of collective union can escalate into witch hunts and lynch mobs. Tribal cultures protect themselves from these excesses through rituals which channel these collective emotions, but not always successfully. Individual tribal members have even less protection from unexpected unconscious shifts in their mood, if these don't fit readily into tribal rituals designed to channel the unexpected energy.

William Golding's classic book, *Lord of the Flies*, offers a brilliant and terrifying example of the excesses of collective tribal behavior. When their plane is shot down during a war, a group of young British boys are stranded on a desert island. Initially they choose a wise leader, Ralph, who with the help of his good friend, Piggy, organizes the boys into structural groups: one to keep a signal fire going, another to explore the island, one to hunt for food, etc. Jack, the leader of the hunters, revels in his task; he appeals to dark fears the other boys feel, and gradually gains control of most of the group. [Doesn't that sound familiar when we look back at the McCarthy era, or the invasion of Iraq during the Bush presidency?]

The boys begin to revert to savagery, inventing a monster–the Lord of the Flies–who has to be appeased with sacrifices. Their fear of the monster lead them to inadvertently kill two of the rational boys: Simon and Piggy. Ralph tries to hide to avoid his own death. The hunters, determined to kill this last reminder of consciousness, set a forest fire in order to smoke him out. A passing ship spots the fire and a ship's officer comes to the island. When he arrives, he finds Ralph lying exhausted on the beach. As the other boys gradually emerge onto the beach, the officer is shocked at what he sees and remarks that he would have expected more of British boys. Ralph begins to weep and that releases the others to tears. As the tears flow, they return again to the children that they should be, though perhaps will never be fully again.

The ability to exert conscious control over our moods and desires is a very great advance! The answer to the tension between conscious and unconscious isn't to deny consciousness, like a Luddite denying technology; the answer is to open a channel between consciousness and the unconscious in some way. Since the two are largely in a compensatory relationship to one another, this necessarily creates tension, and it is difficult for any of us to hold that tension. The temptation is to yield to one side or the another, as we described in chapter 1 as an enantiodromia. If we are willing though to hold that tension, we gradually develop a partnership between the direction and power of consciousness, as well as the early warning system and novelty of the unconscious. Ideally, each complements the other, as in any good marriage or partnership.

Jung terms this dynamic union of conscious and unconscious the "transcendent function" in that it transcends both consciousness and the unconscious. The shadow is the first figure who appears when the transcendent function becomes activated.[47] The transcendent function attempts to restore wholeness by bringing repressed or ignored aspects of our personality into consciousness. Seen in that light, the Shadow is an opportunity for us to grow; this is the position we present throughout this book. If we acknowledge and relate to the Shadow, we grow. If we deny and repress its appearance, it doesn't go away: it grows stronger until we have to acknowledge and relate to it. The psyche is attempting to make us grow whether we like it or not. And, though the Shadow is an archetypal figure, it doesn't take a single form; each of us confronts a Shadow with personality characteristics specific to us. The fact that the Shadow is tailored to fit the individual is an indication that a "transcendent function" actually does exist which encompasses both our conscious personality and the Shadow.

Think about how strange this really is. How is it that at every stage of our development, the unconscious is able to appropriately compensate for our conscious extremes. This seems to indicate that there must be some inner definition of what our ideal self should be, at each point in our development. How else can we account for the fact that when we are near that ideal, our dreams closely reflect our outer reality, and when we stray too far from that ideal, our dreams are at wide variance with our outer experience?

## RETURN OF THE FROG KING: HONORING THE SHADOW

*Fairy tales are the purest and simplest expression of collective unconscious psychic processes . . . . They represent the archetypes in their simplest, barest and most concise form.*

Marie-Louise von Franz.[48]

Perhaps we might end this chapter of the possibilities hidden within the shadow by returning to the story of "The Frog King." When we left the story earlier, once the frog had returned her golden ball to the spoiled princess, she immediately forgot her promise to make him her friend. But the story doesn't end there. Though with his stubby little legs it took the frog a whole day to reach the castle where the princess lived, he finally did show up and knocked at the door.

> When the shadow first appears, we find it so repulsive that we can't imagine that we need to treat it with honor. We try to make deals with it, never really intending to honor those deals. And it is possible to trick the shadow and go on about our lives for a while, as if the shadow will never reappear. But though we think we have been clever, we can't avoid the shadow indefinitely; eventually it will always return, knocking once more at our door.

When the princess saw who it was, she slammed the door and stood shaking with fright. Her father, the king, asked her what kind of monster could so frighten her. She had to admit it was only a frog. When he pressed her, she told him the story. The king, who was an honorable man, insisted that she keep her promise and let the frog in.

> Once we engage with the shadow, there is no going back on our word. The king represents a ruling power inside us which refuses to accept our excuses and evasions. We all come to the point where we must then live with the shadow, despite our repugnance.

The frog then sat down at the table with the princess and even asked to be allowed to eat from her own golden plate. The princess acquiesced, but only because the king forced her to.

> This is our normal attitude once we can no longer ignore the shadow. We would do anything to be free of it, but if that is impossible, we will make sure that we don't enjoy its presence for a moment. After all, we ask ourselves how it could possibly have anything we could ever want?

The meal completed, the frog told the princess that he was tired and wanted to go to sleep .... in her bed! The princess was horrified, but once more complied when the king admonished her.

> There comes a time when the daytime world of shadow projections and the nighttime world of shadow dreams has to join, and consciousness has to acknowledge the shadow in both worlds. Eventually we have to lie down in the same bed together.

Once in the bedroom the princess sticks the frog in the farthest corner of the room and goes to bed, but the frog comes over to the bed, telling her that he wants to sleep on her pillow. That is too much for the princess. She picks up the frog, and, with all her might, throws him against the wall. When he falls to the ground, he changes into a handsome prince. Like many another such prince in fairy tales, he had been changed into a frog by a wicked witch.

> Here we must part with the story as told by the Brothers Grimm. The princess has never changed her attitude, only adapting to the

frog because her father the king forces her to. And it is only through a fit of anger on her part that the frog is restored to its true identity as a prince. Unfortunately, without a change of attitude, there is no possibility of a reconciliation with the shadow. Rather than throwing the shadow away from us in a fit of anger, we have to willingly engage with it until a time occurs when we see it in a new light. So let us retell the ending of the tale in a way that honors the shadow, and what it can teach us.

Though it made her shudder, the princess picked up the frog, placed him on her pillow, then lay down to sleep. Somehow she got through the night and through the days to come, days in which the frog was her constant companion. She tried many times to avoid his company, but her father's admonishments held her to her promise. After some time, she was surprised to find that she no longer found the frog quite so repulsive. Though he was hardly her ideal companion, still she had grown used to him.

There is no avoiding the necessity of simply spending time coming to know the shadow. It takes time to see beyond the grotesque appearance it initially displays; to see what lies beneath that facade. It also takes time for the shadow to develop into company acceptable to the light. As long as the shadow remains hidden in darkness, it doesn't change. Only conscious engagement can cause the shadow to grow and develop.

Then one day, she awoke, expecting as usual to see the little frog on her pillow. But he wasn't there, nor was he anywhere else in the room. "That's strange," she thought to herself. "I wonder where he might be?" When she came down for breakfast, she asked her father the king and her mother the queen if they had seen the frog. They admitted that they hadn't seen him this morning. She told herself, "wonderful, maybe I am finally rid of that frog, and can have time for myself again." But she found the day dragged terribly, and nothing seemed to interest her. She even approached the servants and asked them politely if they had seen the frog. But no one had.

Eventually we come to realize that the shadow has brought something new into our life. Without its energy, life has no zest for us any more. No matter where we look, we can't find that novelty it brings into our life.

Taking her favorite toy—the golden ball—with her, the princess wandered down to the pond where she had first encountered the frog, hoping against hope that he had returned there. But there was no frog to be seen. She looked at the golden ball in her hand and could only see the frog who wasn't there. She took the ball and threw it into the pond, crying "little frog, if you return my ball to me, I'll be your constant companion." But the ball merely sank to the bottom of the pond.

All that we previously had thought most important now becomes of no worth whatsoever. We have to give it all up, but even that isn't enough.

Now realizing that the frog was gone forever, she began to weep and cried: "oh, little frog, I miss you so. Please come back." At those words, the frog came out of the water with the ball in his hands and set it down before her. The princess was so happy to see the frog again, that she pulled him to her breast, and kissed him. At her kiss the frog turned into a handsome prince, who the princess married and lived with happily ever after.

Finally, we have to admit the deep bond we share. And that is enough. Perhaps we don't live happily ever after. Who does? But we do live a transformed life.

*The face we see in the mirror isn't necessarily who we really are.*

CHAPTER 3

# THE FACE IN THE MIRROR:
# THE SHADOW & OTHER INNER PERSONALITIES

Some of the same considerations apply to this inner relationship as to relationships between people in the outer world.
For example, full regard for the other's separateness and idio-
syncracies is essential. In the inner relationship, the unconscious must be permitted to be what it is, and not forced into
ego or external notions of how it ought to behave. At the
same time, the ego must hold firmly to its own reality. This is
as difficult in inner as in outer relationships.

JANET DALLET.[49]

Up to this point, we have spoken of the shadow in the singular, but
really there are many shadows within us. Or perhaps it would be
better to say that the shadow takes many forms. In Chapter 1, we
discussed how, in early dreams, the shadow may take the form of a
vampire or a werewolf, an alien or even an animal. This is because at
this early stage, the shadow seems so strange and unrecognizable that
only such distorted images will do. But it's not as if we dream of a
werewolf, and then that same werewolf keeps popping up in dream
after dream. Instead, a variety of such images occur, not only in the
early stages of dealing with the shadow, but throughout your dream
life. The shadow figures form in the unconscious around the issues
that have emotional significance for you. Jungian analyst John Talley
has commented that: "There are many, probably as many shadows as
there are entities or affects."[50] Over time, different figures come into
existence, transform, melt into one another, disappear, reappear, and
eventually merge into consciousness.

Inner Voices:
the Android and other Multiple Personalities

*...in multiple personality, the skeletal structure of the psyche is laid bare. A window is opened into the soul, and the structure and dynamics of its "internal organs" can be observed in a vividly direct way. The theoretical and practical importance of the phenomenon of multiple personality for understanding the human psych cannot be minimized.*

Richard Noll.[51]

One can see these inner figures most clearly in cases of Multiple Personality Disorder (MPD).* The unfortunate people suffering from MPD have normally had such traumatic backgrounds in their childhood that they have never developed a single stable central personality (i.e., an ego). For most of us, our birth personality evolves over time, from a tiny sense of personal identity into a single all-encompassing ego which forms the center of all of our conscious personality. The shadow appears in order to break up that monolithic structure so that we can add parts of the unconscious into a new structure.

For MPD patients, their birth personality may or may not have survived as the main conscious personality, but one or more (usually many more) other personalities have formed as well. Under varying situations, one of these personalities takes control of consciousness. When this happens, the new personality can be as different from the old as any two people are. The normal conscious personality always remains unaware of these alternate personalities. Because of this, MPD sufferers become experts at rationalizing to themselves gaps in their memory. It is fascinating that usually one of the alternate personalities does have full memory of everything that has taken place, no matter which personality was in charge.[52]

It's easy to see why it would be invaluable for alternate personalities to appear in someone who has an especially troubling

---

* The designation of MPD has been replaced by DID (Dissociative Identity Disorder) by the American Psychological Association. I find the original description better describes the condition as I've experienced it with patients.

*Over time, different figures come into existence, transform, melt into one another, disappear, reappear, and eventually merge into consciousness.*

childhood. When their situation becomes too unbearable, the child simply withdraws from conscious awareness of what is happening and lets another personality take over, one who is better able to deal with the situation. One of the most rewarding experiences of my life was with a wonderful patient who I'll call Rosalyn. She had a "Mommy Dearest" childhood with a mother who, to the outer world, appeared kind and loving, but who, behind closed doors, abused her two children in virtually every way possible. It was finally too much for Rosalyn's younger brother, who committed suicide at age 13. When that happened, a new personality came into existence in Rosalyn, one she called "the Android."

Unlike most MPD patients, where the personalities are each independent entities who appear serially and are never in place concurrently, the Android instead served as an intermediate personality between Rosalyn and life, much like the screeners on radio talk shows who prevent the more disturbing callers from reaching the host. Like Data on "Star Trek: Next Generation" many years later (at least until Data got his emotion chip), the Android felt no emotion at all and only fed a neutered version of reality on to Rosalyn. This protected Rosalyn from her mother's worst excesses so that

Rosalyn survived until adulthood. However, you can't live without full emotional involvement for a lifetime without suffering the consequences. And poor Rosalyn did suffer.

When I first saw Rosalyn, she had attempted suicide the previous week by swimming out to sea. When she was far enough out, she let herself go under and drown—and in fact she felt convinced that she had drowned. The following morning, however, she woke up alive on a beach some miles away, where the sea had gently deposited her. The Android had vanished, never to return. Rosalyn felt as if she had been almost literally reborn. Like any newborn, everything was new and strange to her. This was so pronounced that she would often find herself wondering what even normal objects were. For example, while brushing her hair that week, she stopped and stared at the hair brush, wondering what it was. I was very privileged to accompany her on her first steps into her new life. I'm happy to say that after only a little more than six months of therapy, Rosalyn went back into the world fully healed, emotions intact, having even worked through her anger and hatred at her mother. Of course, a patient like Rosalyn is a gift from the gods for a therapist; I could only be grateful to have watched the process, and could take little or no credit for her healing and transformation. The main thing I was able to contribute to her transformation was a consistent insistence that this process was a good and holy one, not a descent into madness.

Once considered so rare a malady that many psychologists denied that it even existed, in recent years MPD has become increasingly prevalent. This parallels the growth in related phenomena among healthy personalities, such as channeling (of which, more below). The reasons for this are complex and highly debatable and not central to our discussion here. My own guess is that this is one of many signs that the collective unconscious is rising, preparatory to a major change in consciousness.

After the original edition of this book was published, I had quite a number of MPD patients contact me either by letter or e-mail after reading the earlier version of this chapter. They felt "seen" by me in a way that they hadn't by most therapists. I worked briefly with a few of them, but for more than a year with one patient, who I'll call Suzanne. What surprised me was that we were able to do our work together exclusively through e-mail! All I needed to do was put the name of the personality I wanted to talk to in the header of the e-mail and that was the only personality that read and answered the e-mail. Suzanne was an artist who had been able to function successfully in the outer world despite having MPD. The biggest problem she had was that incessantly throughout the day she would hear a little girl's voice n her mind saying: "I'll be good, Daddy. Please don't hurt me." Over and over and over.

Much of my work was with the little girl, who I'll call Mary. She was pre-school age, perhaps 5 or 6, but she could read and write, at least at a primitive level. She didn't want to talk about her Daddy, who was actually long dead in real life. So instead I sent her pictures and asked her to tell me what she saw in the pictures. This process helped enough that Suzanne didn't hear Mary's voice quite so incessantly, but the pleas didn't go away totally.

After working with Suzanne and Mary (and other personalities less frequently), I decided that I had to confront the father. Though he was dead, I realized that he was as alive inside Suzanne's and Mary's shared psyche as when he was alive in the outer world. So I sent an e-mail, asking him to talk with me. He did answer, as if he had no choice, but he was protean, slipping away from any attempt to pin him down. He was as nasty a person as I've ever encountered, but I finally managed to get him to agree to stop hurting little Mary. At that point, Mary's incessant pleas ceased inside Suzanne, though Mary was still alive as a sub-personality. I was never able to fully integrate the personalities, but life was better for Suzanne than it was before. Soon after this we broke off our work, as we both knew this was as much as we were going to be able to do together.

I'll just mention one more thing that struck me as odd during that time when I was being contacted by a variety of people with MPD: I found that there were MPD wannabes. Yes, there are people who want to believe that they have multiple personalities, even though they don't. I had no trouble at all distinguishing people who actually had MPD from those who just wanted to have it. Years later I saw a documentary about Kenneth Bianchi who raped and murdered women along with his cousin Angelo Buono. Bianchi claimed he was innocent because he suffered from MPD and an alternate personality committed the crimes. The documentary included video showing Bianchi being interviewed by a psychiatrist who bought his story hook-line-and-sinker. I was shocked as he was so obviously not an MPD that I couldn't believe he could fool anyone.

### FROM INDIA TO THE PLANET MARS:
### MYERS, FLOURNOY AND THE CREATIVE UNCONSCIOUS

*Between our ordinary consciousness (the supraliminal) and our latent consciousness (the subliminal) there are perpetual changes and fluctuations along their border; the level of separation is not constant; the partition is not impervious; the threshold is not fixed between these parts of our being.*

Théodore Flournoy.[53]

Though virtually all the literature on MPD treats it as exclusively a pathological condition, a view that traces itself back to the prominent French psychologist, Pierre Janet, Jung took a different stance. He felt that the psyche inherently organized emotional issues into *complexes*, which then inevitably took personified form. All change in the psyche takes place through the formation of such inner figures and the conscious ego's engagement with them through dreams and fantasies. Without taking a personified form, there is virtually no way for consciousness to confront these issues. For Jung, this was a natural and essentially benign function of the psyche. As he says: "Consciousness is continually widened through the confrontation with previously unconscious contents, or—to be more accurate—could be widened if it took the trouble to integrate them.[54] In other words, Jung is saying that we all have such inner figures, and that their formation in the unconscious is a necessary first step toward integration into our personality.

Though Jung didn't explicitly acknowledge the debt, he was drawing on ideas first expressed by an older fellow Swiss psychologist Théodore Flournoy, who had befriended Jung during the critical period when Jung was splitting from Freud. Flournoy in turn was drawing on the work of Frederick Myers, a pioneer in parapsychological research. Myers had developed a theory of the unconscious—which he called the *subliminal*—based on his study of phenomena which existed on the border between conscious and unconscious, automatic writing in particular. Automatic writing is what it sounds like: letting writing come out of yourself on its own, automatically, with no conscious intervention. This can be done in any way from using a Ouija board to point to letters, to holding a pen or pencil in your hand and letting your hand write seemingly on its own, to sitting at a typewriter or computer keyboard and allowing the words to flow. As we will see later in our discussion of Jung's technique of Active Imagination, this process is surprisingly easy.

One of Myers first discoveries was the ease with which information flowed during automatic writing. Over one hundred thousand books of such writing have been "self-published or published by vanity presses...in the United States over the last hundred years."[55] Myers found that there was no evidence that the ability to channel such writing was an indication of a pathological condition. He found the unconscious which produced the writing of more interest. "The subwaking self is devoid of all personal characteristics, it is both personal and impersonal . . . . it assumes indifferently all kinds of character and of person, for it has no individuality." In contrast to those who viewed such unconscious processes as pathological and at best subservient to consciousness, Myers found that "the unconscious mentation flowed on intercurrently with the conscious."[56] Interestingly, Dr. Allan Moffitt and his students in his Ottawa, Canada dream laboratory, have conducted extensive research that indicates that the unconscious is continuously active—dreaming—not only throughout sleep but also throughout the day while we are engaged consciously in other activities.[57]

Flournoy drew heavily on Myers' model of the relationship between conscious and unconscious. He summarized Myer's position this way: "Between our ordinary consciousness and our latent consciousness [i.e., the unconscious] there are perpetual changes and fluctuations along their border; the level of separation is not constant, the partition is not impervious; the threshold is not fixed between these parts of our being."[58] That being said, Myers wanted desperately to regard mediumistic phenomena as evidence of our survival after physical death. Mediums had access to the spirit world through the subliminal, to which they had more comfortable access than the normal person. Though fascinated by Myers' concept of the subliminal, Flournoy looked instead for a scientific explanation, rather than a metaphysical one. He wanted an opportunity to study scientifically the details of how unconscious overlapped with consciousness. Like his American friend, psychologist William James, he was convinced that the doorway to the unconscious led through phenomena such as hypnotism and trance. Accordingly, Flournoy searched for some time for a sufficiently gifted spirit medium who he could study scientifically. He finally found who he was seeking in an attractive young Frenchwoman known as Hélenè Smith, who had already become one of the most well-known mediums of her time.[59]

Hélenè had become interested in spiritualism after reading a book on life after death. She soon found that she had a gift and began serving as a medium for the spirit of the famed French writer Victor Hugo. Unlike her modern counterparts—channels—who seemingly allow all sorts of entities to use their bodies in order to speak directly, Hélenè initially answered questions using the laborious, but then common, process of table-tapping. By the time Flournoy met her, Victor Hugo had given way to a figure named Leopold, who was to remain her spirit guide off and on for the rest of her career as a medium.[60]

Flournoy suggested that she allow him to attend her seances and use scientific observational techniques to study her abilities. Flattered by his interest, the medium allowed the process to proceed in directions suggested by Flournoy in order to be able to study the process more scientifically. Flournoy recorded the results of this study in a book that was both highly regarded by his colleagues and as popular as a novel: *From India to the Planet Mars*. The title refers to two key periods of his study, one he called the Hindoo (sic) Cycle, when Hélenè was able to retreat to a past life as a Hindu princess named Simandini and another where she was able to transport herself to the planet Mars and record what she found there.

Flournoy was able to carefully demonstrate that all of the information Hélenè produced in her seances could be explained as the products of her own mind, drawing on a little-known ability of the human mind called cryptomnesia; i.e., the ability to recall facts and events for which we have no conscious memory. Both the supposed Hindu language and the even more detailed description of Mars, complete with geography, culture, customs, technology, and even written language, were all due to this ability of the mind. Flournoy was thus able to explain a supposed spiritualistic phenomena using psychology. It is important to note, however, that though Flournoy didn't have to resort to extra-psychological explanations, he did find himself amazed at the extent of creativity of the human psyche. In trance, Hélenè was able to dictate information week by week, which built up a portrait of complex worlds without any inner inconsistency. For example, one linguist, Victor Henry, wrote an entire book analyzing Martian as a language. He concluded that Hélenè's created language had all the qualities of a natural language. When Flournoy's work is examined by skeptics, this side is largely ignored. It is likely that it was the twin sides of psychologism, coupled with the creativity of the psyche, that inspired Jung's own ideas.[61]

While few of us will ever go so far as Hélenè in making contact with inner figures, we need to realize that we all have the potential to tap creative forces within the unconscious, which take personified form. Engaging with the shadow offers us a chance to develop that creativity.

CHANNELING ZENON:
CONFUSING THE CONTAINER WITH THE CONTAINED

*There remains one last question to pose concerning these new forms of psychological existence. Are they inferior or superior to the waking state?*

Pierre Janet.[62]

In October of 1988, I had a personal experience with a channel that caused me to think deeply about the nature of channeling. I had been reading Jane Roberts' books for the first time. Though I had never had any particular interest in her books before, for some reason I read one of the more personal books, which was filled with Jane Roberts' speculations about her experience of Seth. I found it fascinating. When I tried the Seth books themselves, I didn't find them particularly interesting, but all of Jane Roberts' books about her own quest for knowledge were compelling because she was struggling with much the same issues I struggled with in coming to integrate the shadow into my life.[63]

In the same time frame, I read a book about the Findhorn community[64] that appealed to me very much even though, by any normal standards, the content was sheer lunacy. For example, the Findhorn founders talked to *elementals* (i.e, nonphysical entities who might be thought of as the essence of plants and rocks and anything else existing in physical reality). They asked the elementals what crops they should plant, how to grow them, when to harvest, etc. Though planted in some of the worst farming land on the face of the planet, the crops grew and grew to astonishing sizes under impossible conditions; e.g., 42-pound cabbages, 60-pound broccoli plants, 8-foot delphiniums, and roses which bloomed in the snow.

Another man in the book saw and talked with Pan (yes, the god Pan), fairies, wood nymphs, etc. Yet I found myself believing even the craziest of the assertions because I liked the people so much I just knew they wouldn't lie. Or perhaps I should say I believed and I didn't believe simultaneously . . . . a very handy trick when you're dealing with the stranger aspects of reality. In search of more of Jane Roberts' books, I went to a local new age bookstore. When I paid for the books at the counter, the salesperson asked if I was interested in channels. When I said that I was, he mentioned that he hadn't found many good channels, but he did know of one good one. Would I be interested? I was, so he gave me the name and phone number of the man who channeled an entity we'll call Zenon. I contacted the man—we'll say his name was Ted—and arranged to come to a weekly class which Zenon taught.

The first (and last) session was a real experience. I never got quite straight what exactly Zenon was supposed to be. This class had been going on for quite a while, so everyone but me already knew everything about Zenon. I think he claimed to be some being who lived in many time and space dimensions at the same time, but it is really not significant; whatever his claimed origins, Zenon was a trip! The topic of the class I attended was "guilt". Basically Zenon said that all emotions are only energy patterns and guilt is a useless waste of energy. There was never any situation in which guilt had any positive purpose. Something like that. This was overstated, but was clearly a useful thing for most of those attending to hear. More interesting than the speech was Zenon's ability to manipulate energy.

Ted, an ex-lawyer (at least he said he was an ex-lawyer) made his living now as a "psychic counselor". While trying his best to look the part of the mystic seer, Ted was basically a quiet, subdued person with a fair amount of rather typical occult knowledge. No, Ted wasn't anything special; we have all seen lot of Teds. Zenon, on the other hand, exuded power. At one point, when Zenon had been saying that emotions were merely energy and totally under our control, one young woman said that she had no control over her emotions and didn't understand what he meant by saying emotions were energy. Zenon then did some "tricks" with energy. He turned his forefingers in tiny circles around each other in front of the young woman. She found herself getting very confused. Then he stopped the movement and commanded her to "stop." She was clear again. The men on each side of her also got confused. I was far enough away that I only felt a funny tingling sensation. Zenon then raised and lowered the energy in the room. When he turned his hands palm up and raised them, we all felt full of energy. When he turned them palm down and lowered them, the energy drained away again.

Several times during the evening, when he sensed the energy level dropping, he raised it again. I experienced this as clearly as if he were turning on a faucet. In fact, I would say that I felt the energy to a greater degree than the others. After the class, everyone had a little potluck snack. I talked with Ted and his wife, telling them how excited I was about Zenon's use of energy. I told how I had done something similar, though much simpler, in working with schizophrenic patients. They both gave me some funny looks; I was clearly not their typical student. When I got home and excitedly told my wife about the evening, she said that she could feel energy coming from me as I walked in the door.

The next week, I came at the time I had thought we were supposed to arrive, but which turned out to be a half an hour early. I went directly up to their apartment and rang the bell. There were sounds like Ted and his wife were quarreling, which stopped when I rang the bell. Ted came to the door and said rudely: "You're early, come back in a half hour." I went outside and waited as others arrived. After a while, I went upstairs again with two of the women. Ted opened the door and graciously greeted the two women with hugs and kisses and kind words. He asked me to wait a minute, then closed the door on me. He came back a few minutes later and angrily handed me the $75 I had paid for five sessions. He said: "I don't like your vibes. I don't want you here. Here's your money back." I was shocked and said for want of anything else: "You should at least take $15 for the session I attended." He took $15 and then closed the door on me, nearly slamming it. I was shocked.

All the way home, I examined my actions to see if I had done something offensive, if I had given cause for being accused of having "bad vibes." After I thought it over, I felt sure it was Ted who had the problem, not me. I thought about his reaction to me, both the previous week and this week at the door. After piecing together little hints, I was surprised to realize that Ted was afraid of me; I was outside his experience and it frightened him. What a laugh! A something or other of incredible power was talking through him and he was afraid of me.

That made me start thinking more about the nature of channeling. Reading Jane Roberts, I had found Seth a mite boring, but Jane herself fascinating. It was just the opposite with Ted and Zenon. Ted was a person of pretty average abilities, and probably a little screwed up, as was evidenced by his reaction to me. But Zenon was someone with incredible power, much more power than I sensed even quiescent in Ted. Where did those abilities come?

We have already learned quite a bit about inner personalities in this chapter. In our discussion of Flournoy's *From India to the Planet Mars*, we have seen how Flournoy was able to explain even the most complex creations produced by medium Hélenè Smith through cryptomnesia. And remember Frederick Myers statement that "the subwaking self is devoid of all personal characteristics, it is both personal and impersonal . . . . it assumes indifferently all kinds of character and of person, for it has no individuality." It's all well and good to accept such possibilities abstractly; it is something else again when you experience the power of a personality such as Zenon, as I did. As we will see later, it is still another level to experience such a personality within yourself.

### Channeling Jung: Is Nothing Sacred?

*If we are multiplex beings, let us get the advantage of our multiplicity.*

Frederick Myers.[65]

Nearly two years later, I had an experience with another channel, though at one remove. I came home one Friday evening and found an intriguing message on my answering machine. A man with a strong Germanic accent said that his wife channeled C. G. Jung. He had brought a videocassette of a session which had been shown on Swiss TV. He had already shown the video at the Los Angeles Jung Institute. Someone there had given him my name as a person who might be interested. Since he had to leave Los Angeles the next day, he asked if I might want to see him that evening. How could I turn down such an intriguing invitation? Reading between the lines, I guessed that his reception at the Jung Institute had been less than enthusiastic and he was hoping to find someone who was more receptive.

On the phone, Rene had sounded like a man in his '60s. I imagine I was thrown off because of the accent, because the man I met looked like a man in his early '30s (though he actually turned out to be 40). He was charming and open as he told me a series of incredible events that had led him first to meet his wife, Mirabelle, then for her to become a channel, first for their unborn son, then for Jung. The video of Mirabelle channeling Jung was fascinating. She sat wrapped in a blanket, flanked by Rene on her left and a very proper male Swiss interviewer on her right. She went into trance easily and Rene opened the evening for questions from the interviewer. The interviewer was careful to ask his questions of Jung, and sober questions they were. The interview went on for nearly an hour until Jung (sic) indicated it was time to bring the interview to an end.

Later when Rene and I talked about all this, he told me that Mirabelle was a "conscious channel;" i.e., she was aware of everything Jung said as she channeled it. Jung had insisted on that, Rene told me; Jung said he had previously been channeled through unconscious mediums and found the experience unsatisfactory. This was very significant to me. When Jane Roberts channeled Seth, she was described as becoming a different person with a different voice, personality, etc. When Ted channeled Zenon in my presence, it was like a totally different personality of immense power had entered the room. In contrast, when Mirabelle channeled Jung, her voice remained the voice of a young woman.

She spoke slowly, her face sometimes twisting slightly with effort, as if she were concentrating to read something on an inner screen that was difficult to see or translating words that she could barely hear. There was little rise or fall in the pitch of her voice, and the pauses had nothing to do with the material delivered. It was more like she paused when she needed breath, even though that might be in the middle of a paragraph or even a sentence. I couldn't imagine someone consciously dictating that way without an inordinate amount of practice. The material itself was a strange amalgamation of Jungian thought, coupled with a sort of generic new age channeled philosophy which is heard over and over, especially in the second-rate channels. Freudian terms like "regression," which are used rarely in Jung's writing, were used extensively. Yet, interestingly enough, the philosophy expressed was largely Jungian. One of the most fascinating examples occurred early in the interview. When the interviewer asked Jung what he thought of being televised, Jung, instead of answering directly, used film and projection as a metaphor which he extended to great lengths in a general discussion of the nature of reality. The ideas expressed in this lengthy metaphor, while totally in line with Jung's ideas and beautifully developed in a way that I have never seen expressed anywhere in his collected works, were presented in a manner which was totally different from Jung's normal manner of presentation.

Still further from the Jung of his writings was the channeled Jung's explicit acceptance of positions he dismissed in his writings; e.g. the channeled Jung accepted reincarnation literally. However, he was far less explicit in answer to a question as to whether he was the same Jung we had known as a living entity. There he gave a brilliant answer that would not have been unworthy of Jung. The whole interview was a mixture of such likely and unlikely, pedestrian and inspired comments. It certainly wasn't Jung as I know him through his writings and through the films of him I've seen, but there was material Jung would not have been unproud of, original material. Of special interest in this context, Rene told me afterwards that neither he nor Mirabelle had read any of Jung prior to Mirabelle channeling Jung. As with Jane Roberts and Seth, the channeling had gone on for a while before Jung identified himself as Jung.

This is the kind of thing you either have to dismiss as fraud (and there have been plenty of fraud in the history of both spiritualist mediums and modern channels), or you have to accept that somehow people who know little or nothing about Jung are able to channel information that fits Jung. I assumed the truth of Rene's statement, first because he seemed a truthful (even innocent) sort of person. Second, he was definitely not a bookish type nor, from what he said of Mirabelle, did she seem the type to have dug deeply into Jung. And, of course, if they had, Mirabelle would hardly have had so many non-Jungian phrases in the channeling. Third, if Rene and Mirabelle were phonies who had just learned a few simple catch phrases of Jungian psychology, that would explain the strange mixture of Jungian and Freudian language. But then how to explain the extreme complexity and subtlety of some of the explanations? No, I'm afraid that denying the honesty of the channeling process leads to more, not less, complex explanations.

One is forced to accept that we have access to information inside us which is capable of transcending our normal conscious abilities (remember Jung's transcendent function?). But that inner voice (or voices) is also capable of delivering drivel that we would never accept consciously, unless we thought it was coming from some higher power independent of us. We can set aside our conscious personality totally and let the inner voices have full control, as Jane Roberts did with Seth, and Ted did with Zenon, or we can share consciousness, as Mirabelle did with Jung.

### EDGAR CAYCE AND EILEEN GARRETT

A friend and colleague, Dr. Henry Reed, has also thought deeply on these issues. Dr. Reed has been termed the "Father of the Dreamwork movement" because of his pioneering work with dreams in the 1970's that helped spark the national dreamwork movement (recorded in *Sundance: The Community Dream Journal*). Dr. Reed is deeply knowledgeable about Jungian psychology, but his "center" is the work of trance healer Edgar Cayce. In a recent book, *Channeling Your Higher Self*[66], Dr. Reed looks at the concept of channeling in the broadest sense, covering everything from intuition, dreams, and meditation; to channeled writing in particular, and creativity in general; to trance, group channeling and healing. And much more. In all cases, he looks at these issues with a fresh mind.[67]

One area I found highly significant was the chapter: "Who Speaks During Trance Channeling?" Usually the answer to this is either that other beings are truly speaking through the channel, or that the information comes from the unconscious. As we've already seen, neither stance tells us enough. Dr. Reed begins with Cayce's model that when a person dies, personal consciousness dies also, but the unconscious (which Cayce terms the subconscious mind) survives. Dr. Reed points out that, in looking at what survives death, Cayce makes a further distinction between *thoughts* and *activity*.

> There are the continued *effects*, which arise from the permanent records of all thoughts and experiences—the Akashic Record. Thought are things, Cayce repeated often, and those thoughts live on in eternity. There is also the continued *activity*, which is the soul's spirit journey in other dimensions of being. Much of what passes for contact with the activity of that spirit, however, is actually contact with the *effects of the records* of the entity's experience

patterns in the subconscious regions. That conclusion is one reason that spirit communication is of no use as proof of life after death.[68]

Once we can step away from our normal ways of speaking of these issues, this distinction becomes a fascinating one to examine. Though there is not a 100% correspondence, think of the Akashic Record as the Collective Unconscious (and remember that the concept of the Akashic Record was developed in the 19th century, a little ahead of Jung, so a first cut at the idea). But the distinction between stored effect and continued activity is worth deep examination.

Later in this chapter, Dr. Reed tells about how Eileen Garrett (who was one of the most famous mediums of the 20th century) approached Ira Progoff, asking him to interview the spirit guides she used in her psychic readings. She knew that the two standard explanations were that the entities speaking through a medium were either  actual people who had lived before, or parts of her own personality. "She had serious doubts about either of these standard interpretations and wanted a deeper understanding of her mediumship."[69]

Progoff interviewed four separate spirit guides that Garrett used. He recorded the results of these interviews in a remarkable book: *The Image of an Oracle*.[70] Two of the spirit guides were supposedly dead humans: one a 13th century Arab soldier, the other a 17th century Persian physician. The other two were self-described as gods. Progoff reminds the reader that "the phenomena that occur, the voices, the persons, the imagery, are such that we are not at all entitled to assume that they are what they appear to be. On the contrary, they are symbolic expressions. They are symbolic representations of dimensions of human experience that cannot be fitted into our ordinary categories of knowledge."[71] Here's how Dr. Reed interprets Progoff's findings:

> Progoff learns that questioning them about their *identity* is inappropriate. They cannot give a meaningful answer to an inappropriate question without falsifying the whole topic. . . . Further-

more, he learns that these spirits are intimately connected to Mrs. Garrett herself, and to get rid of them would be to get rid of her, and vice versa. He learns that rather than ask *who* is speaking . . . . it would be better to ask *what quality of consciousness* or level of reality is being expressed at the moment. . . .Rather than think of these spirits as persons, or sub-personalities, therefore, Progoff concludes that it's more accurate to think of them as *personifications.*[72]

Or as Progoff terms them: "symbolic forms of dramatization by which larger principles of life are made articulate in human experience and by which our intimations of meaning in life are made more specific."[73]

It will be well to keep this complexity in mind in all our dealings with the shadow in his many manifestations, and especially in Active Imagination, which is our final topic of this chapter.[74]

### ACTIVE IMAGINATION: TALKING WITH THE SHADOW

*The greatest use of active imagination really is to put us—like the rainmaker—into harmony with the Tao so that the right things may happen around us instead of the wrong.*

Barbara Hannah.[75]

Barbara Hannah was one of the first Jungian analysts, as well as a biographer of Jung. The "rainmaker" she mentions is from a story Jung loved to tell, one which he told her to be sure to use whenever she gave a lecture or seminar on Jungian psychology. Jung said that his friend Richard Wilhelm—the translator of the I Ching and The Secret of the Golden Flower—told him the story was actually a personal experience with a Chinese rainmaker.

Wilhelm was visiting a village devastated by a drought. In desperation, the villagers sent for a rainmaker. When the rainmaker arrived, he asked to be provided with a small hut at the edge of the village where he could live. He then went into the hut and didn't emerge again for three days. The next day it not only rained, it began to snow, to the delight of the villagers. While the people of the village scampered in delight, Wilhelm asked the priest how he had brought the rain. The priest said that when he came to the village, he could feel that it was "out of the Tao;" that is, emotionally disturbed, uncentered. That made him feel "out of the Tao" as well. So he withdrew to the hut until he was once more "in Tao." When he did so, the snow came.[76]

The shadow appears in our life when we are out of the Tao. Our conscious ego position no longer qualifies as a center. Instead we are pulled between its values and a new set of unconscious values which form around the shadow. We have already seen how those values become personified and appear in our dreams. To the extent we make an attempt to remember those dreams, to record them, and to try and engage with them (I won't say try to figure out what they mean because that is less important), we begin a dialogue with the unconscious which can eventually reconcile us with the shadow. But there is another way: active imagination.

Jung's therapeutic method had many different names before he settled on the term active imagination. At first it was the "transcendent function." Later he called it the "picture method." Other names were "active fantasy" and "active phantasying." Sometimes the process was referred to as "trancing," "visioning," "exercises," "dialectical method," "technique of differentiation," "technique of introversion," "introspection," and "technique of the descent."[77]

These earlier terms are useful in that they call up different pictures in our mind of what the process can be. Whatever term is used, active imagination is the process of consciously dialoguing with our unconscious. There are many ways to do this, and anyone who begins the process eventually tries many methods. But two in particular, which we might call the visual and the oral, are useful. In either case, one should ritualize the process in some way in order to set it off from normal life. This is important because essentially you are going to go into an altered state of consciousness,[78] one which will be unique to your particular version of active imagination.

As a parallel example of how one can ritualize altered states to good effect, famed hypnotherapist Milton Erickson often would have two rooms in which he would conduct hypnotherapy sessions. In one room, he taught the patient how to go into trance, and how to deepen and explore the trance state. Only when the patient was comfortable with all aspects of the trance state, would Erickson use trance to help makes changes in the patient's behavior. At that time, Erickson would conduct the session in the other room. Thus the patient unconsciously associated the first room with learning about trance, and the second room with making changes in her life. Of course, Erickson used many more subtle methods of accomplishing the same thing: touching the patient in a particular place at the moment of change, so that touching them in the same place again would return them to the altered state associated with change; changing the tone or pitch of his voice to enforce change; etc.

In Neuro-Linguistic Programming (NLP), this technique is called "anchoring." Many any of Erickson's techniques such as this have been appropriated and systematized by NLP. There is a question, however (at least in this author's mind), whether in systematizing and teaching techniques that were used by a master hypnotherapist, NLP might be promising more than can be delivered by ordinary folks who learn the techniques. When healers are observed from the outside, all that can be seen are the techniques, but healers are more than the techniques they use.

In any case, at least initially, you should establish some ritual of your own for doing active imagination. You can retire to a special room, dim the lights, relax, anything that feels right for you. One simple method is just to sit comfortably, close your eyes for a moment, take a deep breath, and let it out. Then move your awareness to different parts of your body; i.e., become aware of your feet, then perhaps your arms, then your head. After you can readily move your awareness anywhere in your body, open your eyes and begin an active imagination.

Use something previously produced by the unconscious as a starting point; for example, a shadow dream in which you were present. In the visual technique, allow yourself to drift back into the setting of the dream until you can see it in your mind. Then allow the dream to grow and develop, except that now instead of the dream determining your actions, you determine your own actions. You shouldn't try to control the dream itself—you'll find that impossible anyway—but only how you act in the dream.

You should try to behave in a manner which would be appropriate if the dream were actually happening. In a dream, if your behavior is inappropriate to the situation, it is an indication that this is an issue you are not dealing with yet in your life. For example, if someone you care about is threatened in a dream, yet you observe it dispassionately, something is normally amiss. (I say normally because there are no absolutes in dealing with the unconscious; for any rule I might make, I could find exceptions.) Of course, your sense of appropriate or inappropriate may change as you progress in acknowledging the shadow's right to its values. In an active imagination, you have the possibility of pushing yourself toward appropriate behavior that might take much longer to happen if you left the issue to dreams, or to actually evidence itself in real life through projection (see the next chapter for more on projection).

Afterwards (or even during the active imagination), you should record what transpired so that you can review it later, just as you would a dream. You can do this with a tape recorder or at a computer keyboard, if that doesn't distract you, or simply with paper and pencil. If you use a tape recorder, you should later transcribe it into a written form.

Before we move on to the oral method, I want to stress that every single detail that I've mentioned above in discussing the visual technique might be untrue in your particular case. One of the primary reasons why some people do active imagination visually and some orally is that they vary in their major inner representational systems; i.e., some can visualize almost anything quite readily, others almost not at all. Some can readily hold a dialog in their mind, others find this impossible. Still others (and I'm one of those), are primarily kinesthetic; i.e., we feel things in our body. I'm not good at visualizing, and I don't normally talk things over in my head either. Instead my body feels whether something is right or wrong, and subtle body reactions determine how I interact with others. Since most of us assume that everyone must experience reality the same way that we do, these differences in representational systems can cause extreme difficulties in communication. Unfortunately, most systems that teach methods to induce and enhance altered states of consciousness are unaware of these differences and normally presume a visual orientation. Some Jungians, for example, actually presume that the visual method is superior to other methods (largely because that is the method used by Jung himself). But that's not the case; for Jung, the raison d'etre for active imagination is a way par excellence to "distinguish ourselves from the unconscious contents"[79] of the psyche. And that can be done in any number of ways, not simply visually.

But even if you are visual, there are myriads of ways in which you may do active imagination. Jung was able to actually see fantasy characters in front of him, as if they were actually there. Others may close their eyes and see the fantasy unfold inside them. Sometimes you might not be able to see something clearly, but, nevertheless, you have an awareness of what is happening, which advances the action until once more you can see something. There are many shadings possible.

In the oral technique, you hold a dialogue with a dream figure (or multiple dream figures), just as you would with someone in normal life. For example, you can pick a shadow figure who you found especially repulsive or frightening, and dialogue with it. You can actually do this out loud; if so, you may find Gestalt therapy[80] techniques helpful at the beginning. For example, set two chairs facing each other. Sit in one and address the dream figure. Then move to the other chair, become the dream figure and see what you have to say. Move back-and-forth between the two chairs as you do this. You may feel foolish at first, but it takes very little time before that feeling goes away and the dialog becomes real. This is a technique originally developed by Fritz Perls, the founder of Gestalt therapy. Again there are many variations on this theme.

More prosaically (and probably more likely to be used by most of you), you can type at a computer keyboard or use a pad of paper and a pencil, to record a dialog as it goes on. If you are strongly oral, you may actually hear the dialog in your head as you go. If, like me, you are kinesthetic, you will more likely find that the dialog emerges without any intervening sounds inside your head. Since the representational systems often merge inside, these distinctions are not important and in no way should be considered to determine whether you are really having an active imagination or simply faking it, as is the opinion of the more skeptical of the psychologists who deal with hypnotism and other altered states of consciousness.[81]

What is important is that you give free rein, without editorializing, to what emerges from the unconscious. You take what it says seriously and answer as honestly as if you were dealing with a real person. Jungian analyst Janet Dallet stresses that: "Once the voice of the unconscious has been given form, the ego can confront it. It is only from this moment that we can legitimately speak of the process as active imagination, and it is only now that the personality can be deeply changed by it."[82]

This is the step that separates active imagination from channeling, such as we've discussed with Ted channeling Zenon and with Mirabelle's channeling of Jung. Ted and Zenon were two separate personalities, who merely shared time in inhabiting a single body. Perhaps Mirabelle may have gained from her channeling of Jung, since at least she was aware of what she was saying while she channeled Jung; yet still she never engaged actively with the Jung inside her. This need to hold up our own side of the discussion is important because the unconscious doesn't necessarily have all the answers. We have to be like Jacob, willing to hold onto the strangers we encounter and neither accept nor reject their words blindly.

Though dreams are excellent sources of material for active imagination, they are not the only possibilities. You can take a mood, a fantasy element, anything emerging from your unconscious and use it as the beginning point for an active imagination.

> For example, once I was experiencing a very profound sadness, so I had an active imagination with my sadness. Among many wise things it told me was that my heart chakra was opening up to another level, just as it once did when I was first seeing patients. Only this time, the higher chakras were opening up as well. That was why I was experiencing such pain. Knowing that my sadness had a meaning and a purpose made it feel holy; I stopped feeling like an animal in a trap. Life slowly started to once more become rich and complex.

This ability to talk to an emotion like sadness or anger is quite powerful. One person attending one of my workshops was amazed at how easily he was able to do it. He said that he had spent thousands of dollars learning techniques to indirectly get at such emotional issues, when all he had to do was directly talk to the emotion. Jung himself, being highly visual, chose instead to open himself to inner images. Joan Chodorow, who edited a recent collection of all Jung's writings on active imagination, commented that "over time, he realized that when he managed to translate his emotions into images, he was inwardly calmed and reassured. He came to see that his task was to find the images that are concealed in the emotion.[83]

You can even construct a system in advance, in which the active imagination takes place. For example, when I studied Western ceremonial magic, I learned an organizational system based around the Cabalistic Tree of Life, which has ten connection points (called sephiroth) connected by twenty-two paths. There is a complex system of associations—including colors, Tarot cards, etc.—for each sephiroth and path. One does "path-walking" by inducing an altered state (meditation is a good method here), then picking a particular sephiroth or path on the tree to enter (usually by envisioning a door you can open). Because of the web of associations you have already learned to each sephiroth and path, the unconscious has a rich fabric to work with in constructing a world you can then observe and interact with. As you walk different paths through this technique, they build up an intricate web of your own particular associations that ultimately define a Tree of Life unique to you. But note that this can be a merely passive exercise, if you are content to observe without interaction. It is the combination of observation of what the unconscious produces, plus conscious engagement that makes it active imagination.

As another example, psychologist Stephen Gallegos has a personally developed system involving animal imagery. He feels that we each have power animals associated with each chakra in our body. In his system, we address each of our chakras in turn, asking the animal to identify itself, then we visualize and dialog with each singly or in combination. His book, *The Personal Totem Pole:*

*Animal Imagery, the Chakras, and Psychotherapy*, contains wonderful stories of transformation using this system.[84] I feel sure that Jung would have welcomed Dr. Gallegos' system. Jung felt that the land itself has a formative influence on the unconscious. Because of this all Americans have Native American symbols buried deep in our psyches.[85] And power animals are embedded in the culture of many Native American tribes.

Though I've never personally used Dr. Gallegos' system, I have had several indications from the unconscious that it likes to use power animals as symbols, even explicit symbols for the chakras. At a period when I felt under tremendous stress, I had a dream where I was driving down a deserted stretch of road. Up ahead I saw three wolves in the road. As I watched, to my delight one of the wolves actually stood on his head. Later, thinking about the dream, I decided that if the wolf was trying so hard to get my attention that he would stand on his head, I had better talk to him. So I did an active imagination with the wolf. He told me that he had appeared because it was time that he became my power animal, instead of the hawk who had been one for many years. My problems came from being too much of a "lone wolf", that it was time for me to join the pack again. He stressed that I would not lose my individuality in the process, that every wolf, though a member of a pack, was also an individual. Over the next several years, I made a conscious effort to fit in with the pack in several different settings. As I did so, though my life became even busier than before, the feeling of being under stress gradually declined. I was able to share responsibility with others, rather than feeling I had to always go it alone.

These more structured versions of active imagination are rarely mentioned by Jungians, and it is a shame that they aren't. One of the dangers of active imagination is that one can get in over one's head much more readily than with dream work. The figures you encounter within active imagination are normally personified aspects of your own personality. As such, one can engage with them much as one would with people in outer life. But the shadow itself is only partially composed of undeveloped parts of your own personality; it has a collective aspect as well. It can connect with godlike (or demonic) energies that can overwhelm someone who is unprepared.

Most often this takes the form of *inflation*; i.e., one literally gets puffed-up, inflated, with the energy. We assume that the more-than-human energies we are experiencing belong to us, that they are part of our own personality, and we ourselves are godlike. If one's personality isn't secure, it is even possible to be possessed and induce a psychotic state. Jung says that sometimes "the subliminal contents already possess such a high energy that, when afforded an outlet by active imagination, they may overpower the conscious mind and take possession of the personality."[86]

> I used to see this often when I worked with more severely disturbed patients in a halfway home. Of course they were not doing active imagination. Usually they heard voices; they would talk about "good voices" and "bad voices", and had little trouble deciding which was which. But knowing which were good and which were bad didn't make them any easier to deal with. Sometimes the unconscious figures that produced the voices would rise to the surface of their own volition and take control. In one case, this was a demonic presence who usually told the patient to set fires, of which he had indeed set a string. Another would engage in a dialog with his voices, much as we've discussed for active imagination. Unfortunately, at such times, he was convinced the inner personality was an actual outer world person.

Possession is a very unlikely outcome unless one is already struggling to retain one's identity. To the extent that we "actively" (and I stress the "active") participate in our side of the exchange with the unconscious, even inflation is less likely to happen. Nevertheless, we will become inflated many times over the course of any system of spiritual development. Its equal-and-opposite counterpart is *depression*, again a literal description because the energy one normally has available is depressed, pushed down into the unconscious. The cycle of inflation and depression is inevitable if one opens a channel to the unconscious; the key is to recognize as soon as possible that we are becoming either inflated or depressed. Once we do, often the recognition itself is sufficient to center us once more. If not, it is effective to ground ourselves in the normal activities of life, especially those involving physical effort, or those which involve detail, which require our full attention.

I don't want to leave the reader with the impression that encountering more-than-human forces in the psyche is entirely negative. In the 5th century, Neoplatonist philosopher Proclus said that contemplative thought was not sufficient unto itself for enlightenment; it had to be coupled with *theurgy*. Theurgy was the ritual contacting of the gods, by allowing a particular god to possess us briefly. This is similar to religious rites in African and Pan-African religions such as Santería, Voodoo, Orisha, Lucumi, etc. In these traditions, many of these figures would qualify as personifications of the shadow, but a shadow grown so powerful that it has godlike powers. But they are honored and respected, rather than feared and reviled.

Theurgy "is based on the idea that, since the gods are the source of all, the nature of the gods is present, reflected hierarchically, in natural symbols and phenomena."[87] As with my path-walking exercises, someone like Proclus knew so many aspects of the gods that he could go into an altered stated of consciousness and the archetypal energy of the god would flow through him.

Now Proclus was still too early in time to realize that the gods are archetypal forces inside our own psyches rather than physical beings. But we are psychological beings, aware that there is a world inside us as big as, or bigger than, the world outside us. When active imagination causes us to encounter collective personalities who are clearly separate from us, we are able to experience powers and abilities impossible in any other way. Though we must never fall into the trap of thinking that we are that godlike personality, just because it briefly flows through us, there is a part of every archetypal being that we can integrate into our own personality. This is not possible without actually experiencing the god—or the shadow.

If you do enough active imagination, you may eventually encounter a figure of profound wisdom and compassion. This is the figure Jung terms the Self, which we mentioned briefly in the previous chapter and will discuss more in chapter six. Here there is no need for fears about becoming inflated with the power we encounter; it is clearly not ours. Nor do we need to worry about mistrusting anything it might say to us. Sometimes we will first experience this power in a dream, when a voice tells us something, and we know it must be obeyed. The voice of the Self is unmistakable in a dream and equally unmistakable in active imagination. Once such a figure appears, you have a source of almost infinite wisdom available to help you during your development. Until it appears (and it may never), one should remember that the shadow, as distasteful as it seems, is our first presentiment of the Self.

> Even those suffering from Multiple Personality Disorder often still have a connection to the Self through a "rational, usually all-knowing mature personality . . . . The inner self helper is sometimes a wise old man or teacher that claims to be chronologically older than the actual age of the patient." When such a figure is present, it usually mitigates the more disastrous actions of other personalities. Once the inner self figure makes itself known to the therapist, it often "serves as a guide for the therapist and the patient."[88]

When the Self appears directly in either a dream or active imagination, it is an unmistakable moment. But don't talk yourself into believing that the voice you hear is the Self. There are many tricksters lurking in the unconscious with promises of wealth, fame, and power. In that light, remember the story from the Bible of Satan taking Jesus up above the city, offering him all that he could see. Encountering the Self is like falling in love, you'll know when it happens. I would caution that it is wise to remember that even the Self emerges from our psyche. While it is beyond our ability to comprehend, it is not necessarily God with a capital "G" or even a god, but simply the only structure we have available through which we can perceive divinity.

Working within structured methods such as the two I've previously mentioned (i.e., chakra power animals and path-walking), you are less prone to excesses of inflation and depression than simply engaging with figures from the unconscious. As such, such methods are especially useful when one is just beginning to try active imagination. Even within normal unstructured active imagination, however, one can build support structures that are available when necessary. For example, you can ask figures in active imagination if they will be willing to protect you from harm or notify you when there is danger. You can set up some simple warning between you and the unconscious figure—for example, a physical action like your arm jerking upwards—or you can simply let the inner figure use its imagination (if that doesn't seem too inappropriate a pun here).

In this chapter, we have developed at some length the concept that we each possess personified emotional components within. It is, of course, an article of our own belief system, as to how we regard such figures. I am presenting them as possibilities for change, whether they appear in dreams, in projection (see the next chapter), or in active imagination. Most important, we must retain our own responsibility in dealing with them, and not automatically defer to their judgement.

*Projections change the world into the replica of one's unknown face.*

# CHAPTER 4

# THE MOTE IN YOUR EYE: PROJECTING THE SHADOW ONTO THOSE AROUND US

> . . . . It is not the conscious subject but the unconscious which does the projecting. Hence one meets with projections, one does not make them. The effect of projection is to isolate the subject from his environment, since instead of a real relationship to it there is now only an illusory one. Projections change the world into the replica of one's unknown face.
>
> C. G. JUNG.[89]

There is usually little good said about projection; the above quotation from Jung is typical. Critics of projection assume that the person stays trapped in the projection, forever fitting the world to their projections rather than adapting their projections to the world. They believe we are like the robber Procrustes of Greek mythology, who made his victims fit his bed, either by stretching them if they were too short or cutting off part of their limbs if they were too tall. Eventually Theseus forced the same punishment on Procrustes.

Remember that projection occurs when consciousness refuses to acknowledge some symbolic expression which is trying to emerge from the unconscious. Eventually the energy of the symbol is so great that it thrusts itself forth into the physical world.[90] Even so, projection is thus a creative attempt by the psyche to resolve the tension created by the shadow problem (or any other stalemated situation between conscious and unconscious). In all relationships, the unconscious selects, from a nearly infinite gallery of inner figures, one particular personality which it chooses to project out onto someone in the outer world. Thus when we're first getting to know someone, most of what we see is a projection of a figure inside us. As we come to know them better, our inner picture comes closer to matching the actual person. Jungian analyst Adolf Guggenbühl-Craig describes how creative this process is in a personal relationship: "Relationship always involved something creative . . . . To encounter a person creatively means to weave fantasies around him, to circle around his potential. Various images arise about the person and the potential relationship to him. Such creative fantasies are often quite far removed from so-called reality; they are as unreal, and as true, as fairy tales and myths."[91]

We are always projecting; relationship is an active process of throwing our inner world out onto the outer world, not merely a passive pulling in of the world outside us.

This is already a major difference from the traditional view of our relationship with the outer world, in which we are viewed as passive recipients of sensory stimuli from the world around us. Strict behaviorists (and there aren't many left) would then say that the stimuli automatically lead to responses without any intervention within. Most psychologists would say that our minds process the information we read from the outer world in order to come up with the optimum response. But projection presumes something quite different. In order for projection to operate at all, we have to have a highly developed model of the world inside us (and I'm not saying this is necessarily a visual model). Instead of passively accepting new stimuli from the world around us, we continuously project out our best guess as to what we are about to encounter. As long as the stimulus doesn't vary too much from the inner model, we don't have to deal with anything except that inner model. When we encounter something that doesn't fit well with our inner model, our psyche does its best to project something, then scramble to adapt.

So when we are forced by inner pressures to project emotional issues out onto the world, this is merely an extension of a natural process we use in all our engagements with the world. As we will see later in this chapter in discussing perception in more generality, this model of the dynamic between inner and outer reality is science's best current guess at how we actually do interact with the world.

As we discussed in the previous chapter, when we don't deal consciously with emotional issues, those issues gather related experiences around them to form complexes within the unconscious. Because we are human beings whose emotional lives center around other human beings, inevitably those complexes take on human form and eventually become autonomous personalities. Once formed, those inner personalities appear in dreams and fantasies, wearing a variety of outer manifestations, all of which fit the always vague, inchoate personified form of the complex. We examined how we can consciously engage with those figures through active imagination. But if we don't make the attempt on our own, the psyche will! It identifies someone sufficiently like the personified complex to be able to wear the projected identity. In chapter one, we summed this up by saying that there has to be a "hook" in the person wearing the projection, to which the projection can attach (though it might not be a particularly good fit).

But consider what has happened: the emotional issue, previously abandoned in the unconscious, has now found a way to force itself in front of our eyes, where it can no longer be ignored. And in the process, it has brought along all the emotion tied to that complex. Even if consciousness remains unaware of the inner issue, it is now confronted with the problem as an outer event with which it is forced to deal. Since we see the projection rather than the actual person wearing the projection, we deal with the issue as directly as we would in a dream. And, because we are encountering it in the outer world, there is less possibility of dismissing it or intellectualizing it, as we might do with a "mere" dream. And it carries the whole emotional load of the complex with it, which makes things happen in the outer world.

M. Esther Harding, a Jungian analyst who we quoted in chapter 2, pointed out that because a projection is unconscious, it can also deeply affect the person who is the object of the projection. "Here we often see a very strange effect of unconsciousness. For the one on whom the shadow has fallen is unavoidably influenced in the unconscious way by the projections, and if the two people are closely connected, the recipient of the projection may be constrained to live the negative role projected upon him."[92]

Projection can be benign and shared. Psychologist Henry Reed has done research on the connections between intimacy and psi.[93] His general conclusion is that so-called extrasensory perception is, in actuality, an extension of the normal process of intimacy. Or to put it another way, our empathy for someone can easily flow still further into territory that supposedly is limited to psychics. Dr. Reed discussed this in terms of a "liminal zone"; that is, the space that lies between two (or more) people. In any interaction between two people there is always a fuzzy place which is neither the one nor the other, something new formed by their interaction. We have all felt our own personalities dissolve in the liminal zone that forms with a loved one or equally, with someone we despise. It is in just that fluid place that the possibility for change resides. And projection is the first step into that liminal zone.

Projection is the way the psyche reaches out to someone or something new. Jung says that "everyone creates for himself a series of more or less imaginary relationships based essentially on projection."[94] Every new relationship—whether with a person, an object, or an idea—in some way involves projection. In order to fall in love, we have to first project our ideal mate out onto someone in the world. That is the only way to generate enough desire to pull us into a new relationship. As our love progresses, the unconscious is forced to adapt to the differences between the actual person and our inner ideal. Hopefully, our projection modifies to fit the person rather than the person being forced to match the projection, as in the Procrustean bed we mentioned earlier. As we come to know the person better, if the fit is too discordant, then the projection falls apart, and the relationship dies. If the fit is too exact, we may have met our "soul mate", but we won't grow from the interaction, because there is too little difference between the real persona and the previously defined stereotype. When, however, there is a creative tension between the actual person and the symbol being projected, growth occurs. As Jung says "we understand another person in the same way as we understand, or seek to understand, ourselves. What we do not understand in ourselves we do not understand in the other person either."[95] And that need for a deeper understanding of ourselves is, of course, why the shadow appears in our lives.

## PROJECTION AND PERCEPTION: AMAZING ANIMAL STORIES

*The plain truth is that neither in man nor beast are the hemispheres*
*the virgin organs which our scheme called them. So far from being*
*unorganized at birth, they must have native tendencies to reaction*
*of a determinate sort. These are the tendencies which we know as*
*emotions and instincts . . . .*

William James.[96]

Perhaps we need to step back for a moment from the highly personal issues of the shadow to think about projection as a basic process of nature. All perception begins with projection of archetypal contents out onto the physical world. The unconscious stores and processes the perceptions, building complexes around archetypes, such that over time, the complex comes to be projected, rather than the original archetype. Thus we learn to recognize our particular mother and father, sister and brother, to identify which foods we like and which we dislike, which toys are most fun to play with, and so on, ad infinitum. Nor is this process restricted to humans. To the extent that animals are more driven by their instincts than we are, it is even more likely that they perceive the world around them through a maze of instinctual, archetypal projections which unite them with their kin, past and present, in a unified world that is outside distinctions of time and place.

Throughout the many books written by naturalist and zoo-keeper Gerald Durrell are scattered wondrous stories of the innate abilities of animals. Several concern the intricate nest-building abilities of birds. The tailor-bird, for example, actually sews up a nest, using two leaves, cotton strings which it gets from somewhere unknown, and its beak as a needle. Durrell watched a different bird—a weaver-bird—weave its nest upon a slender branch. It draped strands of palm fiber around the branch, then tied them together to form a weave, which gradually built into a nest. The completed nest was so strong that Durrell, using all of his strength, could only take it apart with great difficulty.[97] These birds had to already have the nest-building knowledge stored inside themselves as it was stored in generations before of their species. When the time came to build a nest, that deep instinctual—archetypal—knowledge totally guided their behavior. They project every step of the nest-building process out onto the world, finding what they need. For example, it can't be explicit to cotton strings, since they might find something totally different that would do just as well. That's the power of projection.

Even more remarkable is a marvelous story he tells about red ants warring on a colony of black ants—in order to steal their eggs. The red ants later return to their own colony with the stolen eggs, hatch them, then make slaves of the newly born black ants. As Durrell sees it, the battle plan of the red ants is every bit as complex as that of a human war. Like humans, they send out advance scouting parties that search for possible colonies to enslave. Once the colonies are found, the scouting parties return to the nest to announce their find. During an actual battle which Durrell watched, the red ants used the pincher technique employed successfully in human battles over the centuries. The red ants advanced on their enemy's colony, then split into thirds, with the middle third attacking directly while the other two thirds encircled the colony. The black ants were too busy fighting the head-on attack to notice their danger until it was too late and they were totally surrounded. This was the same technique that famed nineteenth-century Zulu Chief Shaka Zulu used so successfully in his battles with both the British and other African tribes, calling it the "horns of the buffalo."

In this story we encounter all the complexities that are involved with projection. Ants are the supreme example of a collective intelligence; the individual ants carry a minimum of instinctual knowledge that drives their actions. The behavioral complexity of the colony itself, as in the story above, transcends the instinctual knowledge of the individual ant. The colony is able to go beyond the amount of instinctual knowledge of the individual ant because of the ongoing interaction between individual ants and their environment. Psychiatrist, mathematician, and experimental psychologist William Sulis has speculated that the collective unconscious is itself an example of a collective intelligence that emerges from the interactions of the feeling-toned complexes which it contains.[98]

But our ant story isn't over. When the black ants saw that the battle was lost, they tried to save the eggs, but the red ants were upon them. Here, to me, is the most astounding of the events. Some of the black ants fought bravely to their death in the defense of the eggs while others, more cowardly (or perhaps more intelligent), laid down their eggs in front of the conquering red ants and were allowed to survive. It seems incredible that something as relatively unconscious as an ant can make a decision that could be interpreted as either bravery or cowardice. Even an ant can alter its behavior despite being caught within a projection.[99] We might keep that in mind when we are caught in a shadow projection, and tell ourselves it is too hard to escape.

## Mental Models:
### How We Come to Categorize the Outer World

*Mental facts cannot properly be studied apart from the physical environment of which they take cognizance. . . . our inner faculties are adapted in advance to the features of the world in which we dwell. . . . Mind and world in short have evolved together, and in consequence are something of a mutual fit.*

William James.[100]

In the seventeenth century, animals were viewed as machines, the brain as a blank slate on which experience wrote its lessons. To explain their seeming life, thinkers such as Rene Descartes actually drew on hydraulics for an explanatory model, largely because the seventeenth century finally understood fairly well how hydraulic systems worked. By the eighteenth century, electricity was in vogue for science, so of course electricity was used to explain away life.[101] In our own day, the computer rules supreme so it has become fashionable to view the brain as some sort of super-computer, which comes up with logical solutions to problems. Research into the brain has already revealed this computer model to be as far away from reality as Descartes' hydraulic model.

Psychologist William James was one of the first to recognize that the brain is, in large part, a collection of ad hoc solutions to problems. The brain's solutions fit the world because they evolved together. For the same reason, the brains of different species are organized very differently. Brains evolve in order to solve particular problems of particular species. Frogs are interested in worms, so their vision is very worm-specific. Humans are most interested in other humans so our vision is very good at differentiating faces. In each case the brain is structured to best fit our particular needs.

Nobel-Prize winning neuroscientist Gerald M. Edelman argues convincingly that the brain must already have structures in place before it encounters the world, but the structures have to be adaptable structures or it would be impossible to accommodate the variety that the brain finds in the world. Accordingly, Edelman views the brain as a selective system which operates much like evolution rather than as a computational system or an information-processing system. In other words, the brain doesn't have a whole stack of highly structured computational algorithms stored inside it, which it loads much as a computer loads programs. Instead, the brain has a huge number of structures that have been selected over time to solve general problems. They may handle the task at hand, but were not necessarily designed to perform the function they actually do perform. So Durrell's nest-building birds contain highly detailed behavioral templates of how to construct their nests. But rather than existing as programs individually stored in separate compartments of the brain, those templates are stored within the brain's structure itself. And the same components that can be used to tell the bird how to build a nest can adapt to deal with the need for some totally different behavior.

These structures of the brain correspond to Jung's archetypes. How they are used to interact with our environment is, of course, the issue. Here Edelman goes into more detail in essentially describing how archetypes gather complexes around themselves:

> Perception may be provisionally defined as the discrimination of an object or an event through one or more sensory modalities,

separating them from the background or from other objects and events. . . . how, in fact, do we know what an object is? . . . . in some sense, the problem of perception is initially a problem of taxonomy in which the individual animal must "classify" the things of its world. . . .

From the standpoint of the adapting organism, the categorization of things is relative and depends upon cues, context, and salience. Categories are not immutable but depend upon the present state of the organism . . . . Animals can nonetheless *generalize*; that is, an individual organism can encounter a few instances of a category under learning conditions and then recognize a very great number of related but novel instances.

Gerald M. Edelman.[102]

In other words, our perception of the world depends on discriminating one thing from another, then generalizing as necessary. We project out predefined categories stored within the structure of the brain, then modify those structures to fit the task at hand. Those modified structures provide us with new categories that are stored within the brain's structure, using preexisting patterns never intended for this particular use. Once stored, they can, in turn, be projected out onto the world to deal with the same situation in the future.

Let's take a break from the science and think about how this process operates in the psychological projection of the shadow. The qualities that the shadow possesses are already contained within us at an archetypal level. As we refuse to allow aspects of ourselves admittance into consciousness, they gather around the archetypal core into complexes, held together by the emotions we have denied. It is likely that these complexes are actually stored within the brain's total structure, using preexisting pathways. But that needn't concern us here. What does concern us is the fact that there is a mechanism for adapting archetypal, instinctual knowledge to actual experience. When the energy level gets too high, the shadow then gets projected out onto the outer world, using exactly the same mechanism we use in all perception. Because we can't perceive any difference between such projections and normal perception, we experience our projection as reality.

Linguist Edward T. Hall argues that we do the same thing with our tools and other extensions of the human body and brain: we confuse the extension with the original function or object which it is extending. Like our cousins, the primates, humans are by nature curious about their environment and continually try to find ways to extend themselves out into that environment. Tools are the most obvious example. In order to dig tubers out of the ground, we can use our fingers, but if the ground is hard, our fingers can become cut and sore. Eventually we discover that we can use a stick instead of our fingers; we can dig faster and we don't get sore fingers. The stick has become an extension of our fingers. Because this process is so similar to the concept of transference[103.] in psychotherapy, Hall refers to is as "extension transference." In Jung's more general concept of transference and projection, this is a primary method in which the archetype finds expression.

In this regard, Hall is especially fascinated by the work of Russian scientist A. R. Luria. In Luria's *The Man with a Shattered World*, a Russian engineer had brain damage that left him unable to think . . . . literally unable to think! However, he still retained much of his vocabulary. Gradually he learned to shift the process of thinking from his mind to paper. In other words, he found, as virtually every writer has found, that he could think something through by writing about it. His unique difference was that this had become the only way he could think. Luria's engineer could now only think on paper; but consider what that implies about how extraordinarily versatile the process of thinking must be. If the process can't operate inside the brain because those parts of the brain no longer work, it can actually use pen and paper as extensions of the brain.[104]

Similarly, we approach anything new in life by projecting something that we already have inside us onto the world. Initially we confuse the actuality with our projection, but gradually we adapt and something new forms inside us which better adapts to reality. Projection is thus a miraculous process that underlies all perception and all change. We should praise projection, not damn it.

## A Look Ahead

Since the shadow, like any other personified complex, is made up of layers upon layers of personal experience built up around an archetypal core, we may project the shadow out not only in personal situations, but in collective and even archetypal situations. Jungians thus often speak of three separate levels of the shadow: personal, collective, and archetypal. Collective projections of the shadow can lead to atrocities such as the slaughters among the Croatians, Serbs, and Muslims, where whole cultures project the image of the shadow onto other cultures. The archetypal shadow is seen as possessing characteristics that are rejected by all cultures: seemingly evil incarnate! We will talk more about the relationship between evil and the shadow in the next chapter, and collective Shadow projections in chapter 6, but I would like to emphasize here that the projection of the shadow is always an attempt at wholeness, whether done at the personal, cultural, or archetypal level. It is our failure to see our own face in the projection that leads to evil.

*What appears on first glance to be repulsive and evil actually holds wonder and magic beneath its dark face. The shadow only appears evil because of our own limitations.*

# CHAPTER 5

# THE DARK SIDE:
# THE SHADOW AND EVIL

The story is told of some students who came to a nineteenth-century Hasidic master in the hope that he could explain the enigma of evil in a world created by a good God. Reb Zusya, they felt, could do this, for he himself was good and pious, yet sick and poverty stricken.

"How, Reb Zusya, do you explain evil," the students asked.

"What evil?" said the rabbi with wide wondering eyes. The students pointed out that Reb Zusya was himself suffering from illness, pain, and poverty.

"Oh that," replied the rabbi, "surely that is just what my soul needs. Our sages have said, a red halter is fitting to a white horse."

TALE TOLD ABOUT 19TH CENTURY
HASIDIC MASTER REB ZUSYA.[105]

What is evil? Does it have any existence at all, or "is that which we call evil but the absence of good?", as Saint Augustine argued.[106] Or even further, is evil actually good, but we just can't see it given our limited human viewpoint. As Reb Zusya says above: "surely that is just what my soul needs." Saint Thomas Aquinas echoes that view when he argues that "there is a reason behind every evil."[107] The main theme of this book has been the positive possibilities hidden within the shadow. What appears on first glance to be repulsive and evil actually holds wonder and magic beneath its dark face. The shadow only appears evil because of our own limitations, and those are often determined by our particular psychological type.

## PSYCHOLOGICAL TYPES AND THE SHADOW FUNCTION

One of Jung's greatest discoveries what that human beings come in more than one type; there are different psychological varieties of human beings. These variations are probably there from birth; if not, they start very early in life. And there is a structure to these psychological varieties. We are each either *introverts* or *extraverts*, *thinkers* or *feelers*, *sensates* or *intuitives*. Since those terms probably mean little or nothing to you at this point, let me talk about them a bit.[108]

Introverts and extraverts have an equal and opposite reaction to the world. Introverts are more comfortable in the inner world of their own psyche, less comfortable dealing with issues in the outer world. Extraverts are just the opposite, drawing energy from the people and things in the outer world, paying little or no attention to what goes on inside them. I can remember once walking to lunch with a good friend. He asked me what I was thinking about and I said "nothing." He said "no, I really mean it, what are you thinking about." And I said more firmly that "I'm not thinking about anything. Nothing is going on in my head." He had a very hard time grasping this, as there was almost always a dialogue going on inside his head. That's because I'm an extravert and he's an introvert.

Now, sometimes the differences are less extreme. There can be a range between those who are very strongly extraverted or introverted, and those who are less so. But, make no mistake, no one is in the middle, equally comfortable in both places. Probable the most significant difference is simply where one draws their energy from: a quiet, inner life or a noisier outer life. Another simple difference between extravert and introvert is simply the amount of words that comes out of the person; the more words, the more extraverted the person. This particular differentiation is a little less reliable as there are some introverts who have learned to protect themselves from the world with a barrage of verbiage, but normally extraverts are more verbal than introverts.

The two-way split into introverts and extraverts isn't the end of the binary distinctions in Jung's psychological types. There are also thinkers and feelers, sensates and intuitives. Thinkers are more comfortable approaching the world analytically, classifying the world, determining what things mean. Their opposites are feelers, who are more likely to approach events and objects by how they feel about them, whether they are good or bad, etc. More generally, assigning a value to something rather than deciding what it means like a thinker would. Normally, this valuing is done through emotions: feelers react positively or negatively to things on an emotional level. But this valuing can be almost emotionless when needed. Feelers are simply much better at sizing up how important or unimportant an issue is.

There is another split that isn't as obvious as thinking and feeling: sensation vs. intuition. Sensates are totally at home in the physical world; they touch, taste, smell, feel (with their body), and hear better than any other psychological type. They do this so automatically that it is very difficult for them to understand how anyone can deal with the world otherwise. They are very good at absorbing and remembering all the details of reality and are absorbed in the here and now. In contrast, intuitives see less of the details and more of the big picture, less of the here and now and more of the future possibilities inherent in the current situation. One sees the trees and the other the forest, and neither is a superior position.

It's very important to realize that no one psychological type is superior to another. All of us need both introversion and extraversion, thinking and feeling, sensation and intuition. But it is impossible to be fully balanced between all the possibilities any more than it is possible for someone to be both male and female (whether gay or straight). The universe seems to separate us into either introverted and extraverted and then one of the four functions as our *primary function*.

Even that isn't quite sufficient: whether we think or feel primarily, we need something to think or feel about, and we can only get that through sensation or intuition. And whether we sense or intuit, we need to process that information in some way, and we can only do so with thinking or feeling. Whichever we choose is our *secondary function*. The big difference here from the primary function is that the secondary function may at the beginning be only very crudely developed, just enough to allow the primary function to work. Later, we're likely to develop it to a much greater extent. And some of us may develop a third function to such an extent that it's difficult to know which is secondary. But we will never fully develop that fourth function, the one opposite to the primary function.

Jung called that function our *inferior function*; since it was our least developed way of dealing with the world. Instead of the term inferior function, I'm going to substitute *shadow function*, as it seems more descriptive of both its positive and negative possibilities. It's obvious that if we use our primary function almost all the time, its opposite, the shadow function, lies fallow, undeveloped, like ore than has never been mined. But even if we do work at developing the shadow function, Jung argued that we can never fully integrate it into our personality. That's because it is, for better or worse, our connection to the collective unconscious. For better, it offers possibilities that are totally hidden from our normal approach to life; for worse, since it is totally unfamiliar to us, it seems dark, mysterious, even evil.

But what, then, is the place of seemingly absolute evil? How to explain away sociopaths who operate at any level—from private hells like that of Jeffrey Daumer to positions of public power, such as those of Idi Amin or Pol Pot or Hitler? As Jung said: "It is quite within the bounds of possibility for a man to recognize the relative evil of his own nature, but it is a rare and shattering experience for him to gaze into the face of absolute evil."[109]

## WHAT IS EVIL?: STAGES OF MORAL DEVELOPMENT

*In contrast to a given rule, which from the first has been imposed on the child from outside and which for many years he has failed to understand, such as the rule of not telling lies, the rule of justice is a sort of immanent condition of social relationships or a law concerning their equilibrium.*

Jean Piaget.[110]

Swiss psychologist Jean Piaget is famous for his theory of invariant stages of psychological development through which a child passes on its way toward maturity. Less well-known was his theory that were also three inborn stages of moral development:

(1) **blind obedience stage**, in which our morality is merely based on what is allowed;

(2) **interpretation-of-the-rules stage**, in which we recognize that morality is relative to the particular situation;

(3) **interpretation-of-act stage**, in which we realize that we each have to develop our own individual moral values

It is important to recognize that Piaget was not just theorizing. As with his model of psychological development, he developed his model of moral stages based on extensive research with children. He presented children with pairs of stories involving morally ambiguous situations, then questioned them about how they viewed the morality of the characters. Here is one such pair:

(1) John was in his room when his mother called him to dinner. John goes down and opens the door to the dining room. But behind the door was a chair, and on the chair was a tray with fifteen cups on it. John did not know the cups were behind the door. He opens the door, the door hits the tray, bang go the fifteen cups, and they all get broken.

(2) One day when Henry's mother was out, Henry tried to get some cookies out of the cupboard. He climbed up on a chair, but the cookie jar was still too high, and he couldn't reach it. But while he was trying to get the cookie jar, he knocked over a cup. The cup fell down and broke.[111]

The youngest children think John deserves more punishment than Henry because John broke fifteen cups and Henry only one. Older children recognize that John only broke the cups by accident and deserves no punishment, while Henry broke his cup because he was doing something that he shouldn't have been doing. Of course, the moral dilemmas become more complex as the child grows older.

Psychologist Lawrence Kohlberg took Piaget's model as a starting point, and developed a more complex model of the moral stages of development of not only children, but adults. He began with three stages much like Piaget's, which he termed (1) **preconven-**

**tional** or **premoral**; (2) **conventional**; and (3) **postconventional** or **principled**. So far, these are similar to Piaget's stages (though not identical). Kohlberg then further split each of the three stages into two stages, thus creating six stages in all:

(1) **Orientation to punishment and reward**, and to physical and material power;

(2) **Hedonistic orientation** with an instrumental view of human relations . . . . ("You scratch my back and I'll scratch yours.");

(3) **"Good boy" orientation**; seeking to maintain expectations and win approval of one's immediate group . . . . ;

(4) **Orientation to authority, law, and duty**, to maintaining a fixed order, whether social or religious, which is assumed as a primary value;

(5) **Social-contract orientation**, with emphasis on equality and mutual obligation within a democratically established order; e.g., the morality of the American Constitution;

(6) **Morality of individual principles of conscience** which have logical comprehensiveness and universality. Highest value placed on human life, equality and dignity.[112]

The first two stages are characteristic of children and criminals. The middle two are those of the majority of the adult population. 15%–20% of the adult population have a stage 5 morality, while only 5%-10% are in stage 6.

Again, like Piaget, Kohlberg's model is richly supported by experimental data. Most people were found to have a dominant stage. About half their values were at that stage, with the rest of their values scattered between the stages immediately above or below. Both a person's expressed values and their actions were consistent with the stage they were at, though those at the upper stages were more likely "to practice what they preach." The same stages were found in a wide variety of cultures throughout the world. In testing to determine a person's moral stage, Kohlberg used stories which illustrated hypothetical moral dilemmas, much like Piaget had done, though not in pairs. Here is one:

In Europe, a woman was near death from cancer. One drug might save her, a form of radium that a druggist in the same town had recently discovered. The druggist was charging $2,000, ten times what the drug cost him to make. The sick woman's husband, Heinz, went to everyone he knew to borrow the money, but he could only get together about half of what it cost. He told the druggist that his wife was dying and asked him to sell it cheaper or let him pay later. But the druggist said, "No." The husband got desperate and broke into the man's store to steal the drug for his wife. Should the husband have done that? Why?[113]

A person in any stage, even the most primitive, still has to decide whether an action is wrong or right. For example, at the lowest stage, one could argue Heinz was right because "if you let your wife die, you will get in trouble." Or he was wrong because "you shouldn't steal drugs because you'll be caught and punished." By the fourth stage, Heinz' theft would be condoned because "if you have any sense of honor, you won't let your wife die just because you're afraid of the consequences." On the other hand, "if you act out of desperation, you'll always feel guilty for your dishonesty and lawbreaking." At the highest stage, the pro and con argument would merge into a sense that if you don't act, you will condemn yourself afterwards, regardless of how society views your action or lack of action. It is easy to see that our view of what is right and wrong, good and evil, is largely determined by our stage of moral development. It is impossible, for example, for someone stuck at one of the early stages of development to understand an abstract sense of justice.[114]

Jung often said that the shadow appears at right angles to our normal morality. It isn't necessarily right or wrong, so much as it presents a different view of things, that doesn't readily fit into our sense of right and wrong. For example, those who are in Stage 4 believe in the importance of conforming to the rules of the society they live in, the religion of which they are a member. When the shadow appears, it may seem to present them with primitive demands that seem totally inappropriate to everything in which they believe. Yet, in coming to a rapprochement with those seemingly primitive desires, they may be forced to develop a more complex morality in which personal values sometimes have to take precedence over society's values. Often they will be forced to a degree of self-knowledge in which they will necessarily develop a Stage 6 morality in the process. Thus evil perceived at one level of development gives way to a higher good.

Sometimes the morality of the shadow is truly at right angles to any and all of Kohlberg's stages of development. One can be at the highest stage, in which the "highest value [is] placed on human life, equality, and dignity," yet still the shadow presents us with moral dilemmas that challenge our value system. Wholeness demands the lower as well as the higher, a concept that is hard to reconcile with any model that presents advancing stages of development. Still, each of Kohlberg's stages can be seen as broader, more inclusive than the stage that preceded it. There are more possibilities open to the individual, coupled with more demands. Life may be cruel at the lowest stage, but it is simple: merely do what has to be done to avoid punishment. By the time we reach the highest stage, we have to accept our individual responsibility for the collective evil in the world. I was forced for the first time to learn that lesson when I was a freshman in college.

## A YEAR AT TEXAS A&M: I GET AN OBJECT LESSON IN MORALITY

I spent my freshman year in college at Texas A&M University, a then all-male military school. I had applied and been accepted at several very good schools; the only trouble was that I couldn't afford them. "No problem," I thought. Because I had done very well the year before on the PSAT (Preliminary Scholastic Aptitude Test), I had assumed that this year I would do equally well on the SAT and get a General Motors scholarship that would pay for everything. That's the sort of assumption it's hard to imagine making except when you're young and cocky. As it turned out, I did very well on the SAT, but didn't score quite high enough to get a General Motors scholarship.

Now that I didn't have enough money for the schools I wanted, I had to decide what to do. My uncle and two cousins, however, had gone to Texas A&M and had sung its praises. It was a state university and thus, in those days, affordable. For some ungodly reason, that was enough for me to decide to go there. This, despite the fact that there were a number of good and affordable state universities, including one in the city where I lived. The fact that I picked Texas A&M is especially astonishing in retrospect as I had absolutely no interest in a military career. My father had gone into the army before WWII, had gone back to a job in private life briefly before the war started, then was drafted again. By the time the war ended, he was a lieutenant and decided to make the Army a career. So I grew up as an Army brat, and Army brats either become little soldiers or decide that the Army is the last thing for them. I was one of the latter. It helped that my father never, in any way, pushed me toward a military career.

So I ended up at Texas A&M. I knew so little about what I was getting into that I didn't even realize it was totally military! I knew that was part of it, but I was in total shock when I arrived and was issued uniforms, sent to a barber for a crewcut, and assigned to a military company, just as if I was in the Army itself. That's when the fun began.

We lived in dormitories that were more like military barracks with wire-frame beds, military blankets and sheets, etc. We woke at a prescribed hour, studied at prescribed hours, went to bed at a prescribed hour. We marched to meals, ate as a group, exercised as a group, did everything as a group. Only attending classes broke the group routine, but after classes we returned to the barracks, and the regimentation began again. We were totally subsumed within a collective culture. Collective cultures demand that the individuals within that culture subordinate their individuality to the rules and structures of the collective. Military cultures are especially strict in those demands. As we mentioned in the previous chapter, not only individuals, but cultures, have a shadow. We are always dealing with not only our own shadow, but the shadow of the several cultures within which we live. I was to encounter an especially dark shadow in Texas A&M's collective shadow.

It was part of the school's code that fish—as freshmen were termed—were hazed, especially by the sophomores who had gone through the hazing the year before. My particular company, E-2, or Rebel-E as it was termed, kept the school's mascot: a beautiful collie. Thus distinguished, Rebel-E liked to think of itself as the toughest company at Texas A&M. I guess we were: we started with over 60 freshmen and ended with 22, and none were academic drop-outs! The rest left because of the hazing. In most cases, they were smart enough to recognize they were going through torture and to leave. In some cases, they left because they had been broken by the system.

A number of scenes from that year stick in my mind. In one, the company's sophomores had decided I was too cocky for my own good. They told me to wait until lights out, then show up in one of their rooms. When I did, they had me do pushups until my arms wouldn't support me any longer, then I had to crouch with my arms extended—"grabbing butterflies"—until my legs gave out and I collapsed. While this went on, they told me, in graphic language, what a worthless person I was and how I was going to learn to act like a fish was expected to act. Then I would be forced to repeat the cycle. This continued until I threw up. Then back to the cycle. When I couldn't throw up any more, they made me drink water, so I could continue the exercises and throw up some more. Eventually they grew tired of this fun and let me return to my room. Though not everyone was unfortunate enough to go through this regimen, I was hardly a unique case.

We ate all our meals together in the mess hall (as the cafeteria was termed in proper military fashion). As punishment for some unremembered crime, a friend and I were forced to eat "square meals"; i.e., we sat bolt upright, eyes looking straight forward. We then had to pick food off our plates with our forks, moved them straight upward, then back to us at a right angle to eat. If we dropped something, we had to leave the table. This was hardly a punishment, as we also had to drench our food in Tabasco sauce, which, of course, made it inedible. The only other food we could get were from candy machines in the classroom buildings during the day. Though we ate as many as we could, our weight kept dropping off. I can't remember how long this went on, but it seemed like forever.

By year's end I was down from 175 pounds to less than 130 pounds and looked like a concentration camp victim in the school yearbook.

Another freshman in our outfit was a gentle boy whose father had died in the Korean War. He had grown up exclusively among women and, though not gay, was more sensitive than fit into such a setting. From the beginning the sharks sensed his weakness and circled around him. I was just trying to survive myself, so didn't pay much attention, assuming that he was subjected to the same sort of hazing I was going through. But his was worse; for one thing, they made him take his mattress off his bed and sleep on the wire bed springs, wearing a full marching uniform of fatigues, boots, and helmet. I think that lack of sleep was what finally wore him out. He had a nervous breakdown and left one day while we were off as a unit on some group activity.

Once I went to another barracks to visit a friend. As I walked down the hall, I passed a door which was slightly ajar. For some reason I can't recall, I stopped and looked inside. A young man was lying next to the sink with his wrists slit and blood running all over the floor. I yelled for help and wrapped his wrists with towels. As soon as others came who were better able to deal with the emergency, I left. I later heard that he had lived, but otherwise nothing. I never found out who he was or why he had come to that pass.

I remember once sitting in my room unable to stop crying. A sophomore in my outfit who had treated me especially cruelly happened to come in while I sat there crying. He stood there and waited, not unkindly, until I stopped, then walked out without saying a word. I expected the worst, but the incident was never mentioned, and he never again mistreated me in any way.

I did have a few small triumphs during the year. I had to get up every morning and make coffee for one of the upperclassmen, so it would be ready when he woke up. Every day I would fill the coffee pot with cold water, then pee in it before I started it brewing. Seeing him drinking his coffee gave each day a little zest for me.

Then there was the time we "Bab-o-bombed" the junior who was second-in-command of the company. We took a can of Ajax (Bab-o was a similar product of the time; hence the name "Bab-o-bomb") and cut off the metal ends, leaving a cardboard cylinder.

We put a very strong firecracker inside (a "cherry-bomb," I think they were called), leaving the long fuse outside, then sealed up the ends of the tube with tape. Then we waited for our moment. Late one night, when for some reason the junior was gone, a friend and I sneaked into his room, set down the Bab-o-bomb in the middle of the room, lit the fuse and went back to our rooms. When it exploded, the cleanser not only covered everything in the room, it stuck to it, nearly ruining everything. Within minutes, the upperclassmen had all the freshmen standing at attention in the hallway. When asked who did it, I'm proud to say that every single freshman in our company said that he did it. Because they couldn't punish us singly, we were forced to spend our Saturdays marching on the drill field. But we still considered it worthwhile.

Perhaps the most indelible memory was of a junior named Danzheizer. I never knew his first name and don't think anyone else did either. He wore the rattiest uniforms possible and always seemed to be grinning. He hung out exclusively with freshmen, giving them free access to his room, where they played poker far into the night—a rare privilege for freshmen. Late in the year, I heard his story from another upperclassman with whom I had become friendly. Danzheizer had gone through a freshman year much like the rest of us. When he returned to A&M for his sophomore year, he refused to haze the new crop of freshmen. Because of that, he was universally shunned; no one would speak to him except freshmen, who were forced by protocol to answer anyone who addressed them. Somehow he found the courage not to be driven away, but to survive in his own strange way.

Eventually my freshman year came to an end. The next summer, I had a mind-numbing job where I sat on street corners seven days a week, thirteen hours a day, recording when the buses would arrive and leave and how many passengers were on the bus. Obviously I had a lot of time for my thoughts. Two months of the summer passed before I suddenly realized that I didn't have to go back to A&M. I had been so deadened that I had assumed that my only option was to return to A&M and inflict cruelty on a new crop of freshmen. Now that I realized that I didn't have to return, I instead attended the local university for a year where I discovered what it was like to be a normal young college student.

> I was so buried within the collective culture of A&M that I had forgotten that I was an individual capable of making individual choices. I think we often forget that even in the worst circumstances, we have a choice. Even during my freshman year, I could have left Texas A&M to attend the university in my home town. I probably would have if I had only stopped to realize that I had a choice. At the time, I was more concerned with showing everyone how tough I was, and wasn't going to let anyone drive me away. So I was making a choice; in retrospect, an unwise choice. Every moment of our lives is a moment of choice, if we open our eyes. And it is always our choice whether to conform to the values of our culture or to choose to go our own way.

For several years afterwards, I chewed over those memories, trying to make some sense out of them, so that I could make some sense out of life once more. I had never before realized that a collective system like Texas A&M could make normal people do things they wouldn't otherwise. I certainly never thought that any system could compromise my morality. Yet I knew that I wasn't as brave as Danzheizer. I wouldn't have been able to do what he did: to stay there and take a stand against what I knew to be wrong. It's a sobering moment to come up against your own limits.

Clearly there was a dark shadow that lay within A&M's culture. But is there some absolute evil that necessarily lies in the collective shadow of organizations like A&M? If we dig deeply enough into the darkness, do we arrive at evil? Everyone has to make their own decision on such issues, and I will talk about it more in the next section, but for me, I don't believe there is any evil in the shadow, no matter how deeply we dig. And I don't believe there is necessarily any more evil in a collective, cultural shadow than in the individual.

Organizations like A&M begin for good reasons: to teach young men the discipline they need to make something of themselves. But as we have seen before, too much of a good thing becomes evil.

It is easy to interpret the need for discipline to mean a need for total obedience to the rules of the culture. Discipline sometimes requires punishment. Over time, punishment can become so exaggerated that it acquires an independent existence. Eventually the rules of the culture and the punishments which support those rules are ritualized until no one even remembers their purpose. Unless organizations like A&M (and the armed forces, religions, political groups, businesses, etc.) constantly examine their own process, the shadow will force itself to the surface in a necessary balance to the distorted view that the culture has of itself. The price of success in achieving balance, whether in an individual or a group, is vigilance.

### TOLKEIN'S THE LORD OF THE RINGS: AN EPIC BATTLE BETWEEN GOOD AND EVIL

*Three rings for the Elven-kings under the sky,*
*Seven for the Dwarf-lords in their halls of stone,*
*Nine for Mortal Men doomed to die,*
*One for the Dark Lord on his dark throne*
*In the land of Mordor where the Shadows lie,*
*One Ring to rule them all, One Ring to find them,*
*One Ring to bring them all and in the darkness bind them*
*In the Land of Mordor where the Shadows lie.*

J. R. R. Tolkein.[115]

J. R. Tolkein's *The Lord of the Rings* is an epic story of the battle between good and evil for possession of the earth and the souls of those who inhabit it. In presenting this struggle, Tolkein is wise enough never to show the ultimate source of evil: the dark wizard Sauron. Throughout the nearly 1,500 pages of this story, we encounter only relative evil, characters who, though frightening in themselves, serve as pale reflections of Sauron's evil. There are the Black Riders, once mighty warriors, who succumbed to the temptation to wear rings of power offered by Sauron. This gave them immortality but at the cost of their humanity. They are now the undead—"ringwraiths"—who fly through the air on wicked steeds to swoop down on those who oppose Sauron. Or Saruman the White, a mighty wizard who had once fought against Sauron's evil, but who lost his own battle with the sin of pride and became merely another of Sauron's servants. As we encounter these and other frightening figures throughout the story, we constantly find ourselves asking then what is the evil of Sauron like, that these may be only pale imitations? Perhaps that is the only way we mere humans can ever approach absolute evil as something that must have existence in order for us to encounter its manifestations throughout the world.

Because evil is thus presented as the backdrop against which the heroes struggle, we see over and over again the complexity of the relationship between good and evil. Each time, in some way the One Ring, the greatest of the Rings of Power, serves as the focal point for the struggle between good and evil. On one side are all of Sauron's seemingly invincible forces. On the other, the Fellowship of the Ring, composed of nine companions: the wizard Gandalf; two men, Boromir and Aragorn (also known as Strider); Legolas the elf; Gimli the dwarf, and four little Hobbits, Merry, Pippin, Frodo Baggins, and his servant and companion Samwise Gamgee. Perhaps because only the smallest and least can bear such a burden, the One Ring is borne by Frodo. It proves a heavy burden and a strong temptation for all.

For example, Boromir wants only to accomplish what he regards as the good: to protect his people against Sauron's forces of evil. Surely, he believes, a mighty warrior such as himself is the proper person to possess the One Ring—someone who would know how to make use of its power, not a weak, silly little creature like the Hobbit Frodo. Boromir's failure to recognize the destructive temptations of power leads him to try to kill Frodo in order to steal the ring. By chance, Frodo slips on the ring, finds that he has become invisible, and makes his escape, later to be rejoined by his faithful companion Sam (short for Samwise). Boromir's actions thus split the companions of the ring for the first of several times into separate groups, never to be rejoined until the completion of the tale. Boromir atones for his sin of pride by sacrificing himself to allow two other Hobbits, Merry and Pippin, to escape the orcs (more commonly known in other mythological tales as goblins).

Pride and arrogance is a common starting place for many of us on the journey, as it was for Boromir (and for Ged!) I know it was for me in my life, as I've told in chapter one. I had been raised to feel that I had special gifts and, concomitantly, special responsibilities toward others. This twin combination had already led me to my youthful philosophy that "there ARE relative values!" I struggled with my values and felt they had extra weight because of that struggle. For me, the shadow had to slowly take me down one peg at a time, until I finally realized that everyone has to struggle with their values, that everyone has special gifts and responsibilities, that everyone's life is worth as much as my own life. It is one thing to care for others from a privileged position, quite another to care about each and every one of them because we are all in the same boat together.

A wiser example is the wizard Gandalf the Grey, whose very title expresses the ambiguity of his moral position. Seemingly arrogant and ill-tempered and someone to avoid, he, instead for the first half of the journey, serves as the moral compass for the rest of the fellowship of the ring. He is grey because he recognizes the complexity of the mixture of good and evil in all our actions. Gandalf could himself have taken the ring before Frodo ever began the journey, but he is wise enough to realize that no one is capable of using such power without succumbing to its temptations.

But wizards are very old, living hundreds, if not thousands, of years. It is very difficult for any of us to come to realize our own limits within our short span of three-score-and-ten. Instead the shadow comes to us to present us with our limits. We need to greet it as a welcome friend.

Each of the members of the quest serves in some way as a touchstone for the shifting balance between good and evil in the story. But more than anyone else, the Hobbits Frodo and Samwise and the once-Hobbit Gollum, show us how complex the balance between good and evil actually is. Since no one is wise enough to wear the ring, it must be destroyed. Yet it can only be destroyed by casting it into the fires of the volcanic Mount Doom, in which

*But wizards are very old, living hundreds, if not thousands, of years.
It is very difficult for any of us to come to realize our own limits within
our short span of three-score-and-ten. Instead the shadow comes to us to
present us with our limits. We need to greet it as a welcome friend.*

it was originally forged. And Mount Doom lies in the middle of Mordor—the dark land—the heart of Sauron's evil kingdom. So while the other companions of the ring have great adventures and fight great battles, Frodo and Sam must simply plod deeper and deeper into what Conrad called "the heart of darkness."

It is impossible to deal with evil by mere avoidance, one has to visit the dark lands, go to the edge of doom itself. We saw this in Ged's story, and we see it in our own lives. I remember when I was working as a counselor and night manager at a halfway home for severely disturbed young adults. I'd get up before any of the residents and spend the early hours of the morning in the kitchen with "Nick the Cook." I never knew him by any other name. Nick had been a heroin addict. He beat heroin by using cocaine. Then he beat cocaine by using booze. Finally he beat booze by using Alcoholics Anonymous. I don't know much about AA, but Nick told me they believe that we all have a dark place inside our soul, and we have to pass through that dark place in order to become whole. That's been my experience. No one can come to wholeness without coming to terms with darkness.

Several times along the way, Frodo is forced to slip the ring on his finger in order to become invisible and escape detection. Each time, his gain is also his loss because the ring gains some power over him, tempting him to covet the ring for himself. He fights that temptation with all his will. By the latter part of the journey, Frodo is so worn by both physical wounds and the draining power of the ring that he can no longer even walk.

"I can't manage it, Sam," he said. "It is such a weight to carry, such a weight."[116]

When Sam offers to carry the ring for him, Frodo's avarice takes over and he refuses, for a brief moment afraid that Sam is trying to take his precious ring from him, before he realizes that Sam is only trying to help him.

"No, no, Sam," he said sadly. "But you must understand. It is my burden, and no one else can bear it."[117]

Each of us in some way comes to a point in our lives, where we realize that no one else can bear our burden, no matter how much they love us. This is the loneliest place on our journey, but also in some way the beginning of the last stage of the journey. Only someone who has struggled with the shadow can come to this recognition.

Frodo and Sam toss away everything else they carry in order to lighten their load. But the weight of the ring grows ever heavier. Finally Frodo can go no further. So Sam, unable to carry the ring for Frodo, carries Frodo.

Sam looked at him and wept in his heart, but no tears came to his dry and stinging eyes. "I said I'd carry him, if it broke my back," he muttered, "and I will!"

"Come, Mr. Frodo!" he cried! "I can't carry it for you, but I can carry you and it as well. So up you get! Come on, Mr. Frodo dear! Sam will give you a ride. Just tell him where to go, and he'll go."[118]

There are few scenes in literature so touching as that of Sam struggling forward, bearing the full weight of his master Frodo, who in turn is nearly unconscious from carrying the moral weight of the ring. This marks the point where we know that only we can carry our burden, yet we no longer have the strength to do it alone. At that point, we find that if we are willing to give up our last vestiges of pride, there are loved ones who can carry us, even as we carry our burden. Even when there is no actual person around us to serve that function, we will find within us a force, humble and probably taken for granted, that can support us during these most difficult of all times.

Sam carries Frodo as far as he can. When even brave Sam can go no further, Frodo finds he has the strength to crawl. Somehow he comes to the edge of the mighty volcano—the point of his destiny where he must destroy the One Ring. And he finds the ring has won. Carrying it for so long, wearing it so often, now that the time has come, he can't part with it.

"I have come," he said. "But I do not choose now to do what I came to do. I will not do this deed. The Ring is mine!" And suddenly, as he set it on his finger, he vanished from Sam's sight.[119]

Just at that moment, when it seems all has been for naught, Gollum appears. We talked of Gollum in chapter one, as an example of how we have to deal with the shadow at its most repulsive. Gollum, once a Hobbit, had found the ring and, under its influence, had evolved into a repulsive, slimy creature, nearly eternal but condemned to live hidden away in caverns, far from the light. As you may recall, Frodo's uncle Bilbo Baggins cheated Gollum out of the ring and managed to get away. That forced Gollum out of his caves to hunt by night for the ring. Eventually he finds Frodo. Sam wants to kill Gollum; instead Frodo treats Gollum with firmness, but with charity as well. Gollum serves as their guide to Mordor until, due to his treachery, Frodo and Sam are forced to leave him and go on alone.

But Gollum has continued to track them and now jumps on the invisible Frodo, fighting for possession of the ring. After a bitter struggle, Gollum bites off Frodo's ring finger, and holds finger and ring aloft in triumph. But in his struggle, he has moved too close to the edge of the volcano and falls in. Thus the ring is finally destroyed. Once destroyed, Sauron's power are gone, and the darkness he has lived with so long lifts off Frodo. Characteristically, the first thing Sam thinks of is Frodo's "poor hand" and the first Frodo thinks of is Gollum.

> "Do you remember Gandalf's words: *Even Gollum may have something yet to do.* But for him, Sam, I could not have destroyed the Ring. The Quest would have been in vain, even at the bitter end. So let us forgive him. For the Quest is achieved, and now all is over. I am glad you are here with me. Here at the end of all things, Sam."[120]

The shadow is a necessary guide along the way, even if there is a part of it which can, and should, never be integrated into our consciousness because it belongs in the darkness. The challenge of the shadow is not to try evil in order to become whole. Beyond the relative evil that can transmute into gold may, in fact, lie true evil. And we must never yield to that. Yet still, it is far wiser if we refrain from judging it, for we may find that even evil may yet serve a purpose in our lives . . . . like Gollum.

It would seem that the story ends here, but this is a very wise story and there is still one further lesson it has to teach us. With the Ring destroyed and Sauron's evil dispersed, the tale is filled with triumphs and celebrations. Aragorn becomes king and has a grand wedding. When the Hobbits return to their beloved land, the Shire, they find that evil humans are running things. After what they have gone through, Merry and Pippin, the youngest of the Hobbits, have little trouble righting things again. Sam returns to his loved one, Rosie, to marry and live happily ever after.

But with the destruction of the ring, not only Sauron's evil has died, but an age has died, the Third Age when elves and wizards still lived on Middle Earth, as the world was called. Gandalf and the elves prepare to sail away from Middle Earth, to leave the world as we know it. And Frodo goes with them. For there is no place left for Frodo among normal Hobbits and humans. He has seen too deeply into the darkness and can never again feel well and healthy in the normal world. Nor, for that matter, will he be wholly at home even at the destination where Gandalf and the elves must go. Frodo has passed beyond living anywhere except inside himself.

*The collective Shadow can be carried by everyone in a race, culture, or nation. It breeds fear, hatred, and distrust.*

CHAPTER 6

# THE COLLECTIVE SHADOW:
## THE SHADOW IN THE WORLD AROUND US

Toward the autumn of 1913 the pressure which I had felt
was in *me* seemed to be moving outward, as though there
were something in the air. The atmosphere actually seemed
to me darker than it had been. It was as though the sense of
oppression no longer sprang exclusively from a psychic situation, but from concrete reality. This feeling grew more and
more intense.

C. G. JUNG.[121]

Up to now, we've largely talked about the Shadow as it appears in
an individual to reflect issues in their individual life. Sometimes the
appearance has been collective, in that the issues raised come from
archetypal roots rather than the person's individual life. But we haven't
looked at how the shadow is projected collectively in the world, or
how a collective shadow appears in the dreams and visions of those
most sensitive to early warnings from the unconscious.

### JUNG'S FRIGHTENING DREAMS & VISIONS PRESAGING WWI

Jung and Freud split in 1913 after the publication of Jung's book
*The Psychology of the Unconscious*[122], in which Jung presented a view
of the unconscious sharply at odds with Freud's. Where previously
Jung had been publicly anointed by Freud as his successor, in charge
of conferences and journals, now he was excommunicated, out on
his own. He still had colleagues in Switzerland, but his world had
suddenly shrunk just at a point in the time when he had expected it
to grow. He was thrown into himself in a way that he hadn't expe-

rienced before. He began having terrifying dreams and visions. In October of that year, he had a vision in which he saw all the low-level countries in Europe covered by a flood. In his native Switzerland the mountains kept growing higher in an attempt to stay above the flood. He could see thousands of drowned bodies floating below him. Then finally this awful sea turned to blood. This vision went on for a full hour and left him weak and confused.

After two weeks, the vision occurred again, but this time the sea was even bloodier. This time he heard an inner voice which told him that this was all real and would happen, that he could not doubt it. We have already talked about the voice of the Self, the voice that can't be disbelieved. But Jung was not yet ready to believe that his visions were of the great world war that was soon to come; he chose instead initially to interpret them as reflecting a possible psychosis forming in reaction to his newly vulnerable state.

In 1914, he had a dream that continued this theme, a dream that recurred three times, in April, May and June. This time, rather than a flood destroying the world, a wave of ice descended from the Arctic, freezing everything in its path. Everything green was destroyed by the frost and there was not a single human being left to be seen. In the last of the three reoccurrences of the dream, there was, however, one positive sign: "There stood a leaf-bearing tree, but without fruit (my tree of life, I thought), whose leaves had been transformed by the effects of the frost into sweet grapes full of healing juices. I plucked the grapes and gave them to a large waiting crowd."[123]

Then in August the world war broke out. Though all wars are awful, WWI changed the face of the world in a way that no other war of modern times ever did. Fully a quarter of the British and European soldiers who fought in the war either died or were permanently disabled, and another quarter were severely injured. The British and Europeans were left with their best and brightest young men sacrificed for nothing. The empires that had joined forces either to extend or defend their domains were largely destroyed, left as a relic of history. One positive change, perhaps related to Jung's tree, was that a class system that had survived virtually intact since the Middle Ages, was also left in ruins. A new world was forced to

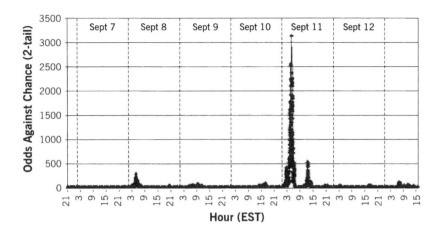

rebuild from those ruins, only to begin a still greater war barely two decades later.

## The Global Consciousness Project & 9/11 Suicide Attacks

So a horrendous flood of blood was indeed on the horizon, and Jung was one of those whose psyche was itself flooded by those future visions of a shadow that was appearing in the world. In more recent times, the single event that probably had an emotional impact on the greatest number of people throughout the world was probably the Al-Qaeda suicide plane attacks on the twin towers in New York City on Sept. 11, 2001. Nearly 3,000 people from over 70 different countries died as a result of the attacks. Though many more have died in war related incidents in recent years, almost all who died on 9/11 were innocent civilians with no interest in any conflict. And rather than being merely some atrocity that we read about in the paper or on the internet and then forget, this event happened in real time on television where people from all over the world could watch it. And watch it over and over, endlessly over the next several days. It united the world in grief, including many people from countries who normally have an antipathy toward America.

World War I lasted almost five years, and Jung's presaging visions occurred over most of the previous year. In contrast, the events of

9/11 took place over less than two hours on a single morning (8:46 a.m. to 10:48 a.m.), and presentiments of this event had an effect not simply on sensitive individuals as with Jung's, but on huge numbers of people throughout the world two and a half hours earlier. There is clear evidence for this, but in order to understand this strange evidence, we need to learn a little bit about the Global Consciousness Project (GCP). Two scientists, Dean Radin of the Institute for Noetic Sciences and Roger Nelson of Princeton University made the assumption that critical events in the world would be likely to affect the consciousness not only of individual human beings, but of large numbers of people who might not even be aware that they were being affected. Previously tests of psi abilities examined the ability of people to affect the results of random number generators. Radin and Nelson speculated that if enough people were impacted by a global event, the change in their consciousness would in turn affect the results of tiny random number generators, leading to non-random results that would have no other explanation.

To test this theory, beginning in 1997, under their direction, tiny electronic random number generators were placed around the world; on 9/11/01 there were 37 of them in place, 65 at this time. Two hundred times every second, each device generated a computer "bit" (i.e., either a zero or a one.) This results are transmitted in parallel over the web to computers that track the bits and analyze them for unusual results. Under normal circumstances, each random number generator should generate roughly an equal number of zeros and ones each second. The GCP had the results fed automatically into a computer program that analyzed how statistically significant or insignificant the difference of the actual results were from the expected results.

Beginning several hours before the suicide bombings on 9/11, and peaking at 6:10 a.m., two and a half hours before the attacks, the results swung widely from expected. The odds of such results occurring were over 3,000 to 1. A second spike with odds of over 600 to 1 occurred several hours later, after the attacks were complete. It's much easier to grasp what this means when you see a chart that shows the results over several days before and after 9/11.

This chart is reproduced with the permission of Dean Radin of the Institute of Noetic Sciences. In a private email he told me that: "What is more impressive to me than just the 9/11 result are the cumulative results of testing 317 events of large-scale interest. The odds against chance of that database are now approaching a billion to one."[124] Those who want to know more about the history, methodology and on-going results of the Global Consciousness Project should go to their web site at: http://noosphere.princeton. edu/index.html.

## PROJECTING THE SHADOW ONTO GROUPS AND NATIONS

In the next chapter, I'll present three different versions of the stages in which projections are withdrawn and the Shadow integrated at the personal level. I'm going to anticipate myself and discuss one of those models: Jungian analyst Wolfgang Giegerich's five stages for the process of integrating the Shadow. I'm using his in particular because the names of the first three stages are drawn from classic situations, in which the Shadow is contained within a group, or even a nation, and projected out onto another group or nation.

(1) the **Enemy or Crusade Stage** (in which the enemy is definitely outside us, different from us. This stage is characterized by fear);

(2) the **Heretic or Witch-Hunt Stage** (in which enough of the projection has been withdrawn that we now find the enemy among us. This stage is associated with condemnation);

(3) the **Turncoat or Subversive Stage** (in which the shadow "is wherever there is light, also in me." This stage is associated with cynicism);

(4) the **Mea Culpa Stage** (in which the existence of the shadow within our self is fully acknowledged. This stage is characterized by guilt);

(5) the **Hospitality Stage or the Accomplished Integration.**[125]

I think we can readily see at least the early stages in operation in the conflicts in the world around us. Unfortunately, I think we can confine ourselves to examples of the first three stages, as I don't see much evidence of advancement to the last two stages of integration in world issues. We can deal with them in the next chapter when we discuss integration of the Shadow at a personal level. Let's begin with the first stage, the Enemy or Crusade Stage, which is where most of the Shadow issues are in the world at any given time.

The Crusades were an attempt to recover Christian control of the Holy Land from the "infidels;" though the enemies were largely the Muslims, they also included a wide variety of "pagans;" including Slavs, Jews, Greek Orthodox Christians, etc. The original Crusades lasted two hundred years from late in the 11th century to nearly the 14th century, though other abortive attempts took place on through to the 15th century.

Though fueled by the religious zeal of the Crusaders themselves, and of course, equally by the "infidels" they fought, there were powerful players behind the scenes who pushed for the Crusades in order to accomplish larger political needs that often overshadowed the religious reasons. For example, the first five Crusades were all sanctioned by the varied Popes of the time; the first was in part a way of siphoning off a large number of marauding soldiers with very little to do except cause trouble in Europe. And, of course, all of the Crusades provided a way to win the hearts of the general population yearning for some great cause with which they could demonstrate their piety.

Perhaps the saddest of the Crusades was the so-called Children's Crusade of 1212. Supposedly a little boy, either French or German depending on the story, had visions much like Joan of Arc two centuries later, in which Jesus appeared and told the boy to lead a crusade of children who would peacefully convert the Muslims to Christianity. Preaching and performing miracles, he moved through Europe on his way to the Mediterranean Sea, gathering an "army" of 30,000 children along the way. Once there, the sea was supposed to part, allowing the children to walk to Jerusalem. Even in the legends, this didn't happen; instead two "kindly" merchants offered the children safe passage to the Holy Land. Once on the boats, however, they were taken to Tunisia and sold into slavery, or else died in a shipwreck along the way. Though the entire story is now largely viewed as fiction, we can view it as an example of the collective psyche pushing forth the most extreme contrast between evil and innocence, with the ungodly infidels on one side and the innocent children on the other.

Most of those who participated in the Crusades on either side were stuck in Stage 1, fully believing in the evil of their enemies, the righteousness of their cause. We can readily see also the cynicism of Stage 3, the Turncoat Stage, in the behind-the-scenes maneuvering which started the Crusades and kept them alive for so long; and, of course, most clearly in the story of the merchants who sold the children into slavery.

The Crusades drew their strength from the sense of moral superiority and the knowledge that "god was on their side," a belief that has been used to support virtually every war and every atrocity in history. The best breeding ground for collective Shadow issues to appear is in those who have little self-awareness coupled with a deep need to fulfil a divine purpose. Let's turn to a modern example: ex-president George W. Bush. As a young man, Bush was a lackluster student who struggled with alcohol and possibly cocaine problems. He failed at most of the jobs that he tried, even though supported richly by family money. Desperately needing something to sustain him, he turned to religion: a simple, clear-cut version of religion. In 1985, a good friend persuaded him to join a weekly Bible study group. It was good for him as it led him to straighten up his life. His first real success in business came afterwards when he was managing general partner of the Texas Rangers baseball team. But it prepared a ripe field for cultivation of a collective Shadow, as he began to believe that God had a divine purpose for his life; that can be a wonderful thing in many lives, but a frightful one when it's coupled with too much power, scant self-awareness, and a desire for overly simplistic solutions to complex issues.

By 1994, he had become governor of Texas, defeating the popular governor Ann Richards, in part by vowing to allow Texans to carry concealed weapons (which Richards had vetoed), and in part because of a political campaign which spread a rumor that Richards was a lesbian. The latter is the classic technique of vilifying an opponent used by unscrupulous politicians throughout the ages; e.g., Richard Nixon won his senate seat with a cynical campaign in which he said that his opponent, Democratic Representative Helen Gahagan Douglas, was "pink right down to her underwear."[126] In Bush's case though, it is more likely that he already felt he was following path prepared for him by God and thus anything he did to advance along that path was God's will. By the time of his run for the presidency, he was explicit about this; he is reported to have told minister James Robison that "I've heard the call. I believe God wants me to run for President."[127]

In the first year of his presidency, it seemed clear that he was overmatched by his job. Then 9/11 happened. There is nothing like a war with a clearly defined opponent to bring out the Shadow. For Bush, the complex situation which produced the on-going strife in the Middle East and then the tragedy of 9/11 was quite simple: bad guys vs. good guys, with no shading in between. This is characteristic of Shadow projection. Soon after 9/11, when he was asked by a reporter if he wanted Bin Laden dead, he replied with typical Wild West bravado: "I want justice. And there's an old poster out West, I recall, that says, 'Wanted: Dead or Alive.'"[128] That same day, on the White House Lawn, he actually used the word "crusade," calling his mission "this crusade, this war on terrorism."[129] In his mind, he had found why God wanted him to be president. Within months, his Shadow projections spread beyond Bin Laden and Al Qaeda, onto Saddam Hussein in Iraq: "after all, this is the guy who tried to kill my dad."[130] In his mind, and increasingly in his rhetoric, Bin Laden and Saddam Hussein were inextricably linked; after all, if we were the good guys, then everyone against us were the bad guys. Within a year and a half, he had invaded Iraq. He turned from his pursuit of Bin Laden at a time when it might have been possible to destroy Al Qaeda and locate Bin Laden, because he viewed Saddam Hussein as even more dangerous. After all, he was convinced that Saddam Hussein had WMD's (weapons of mass destruction). The messianic tone was in full force when he forced the invasion of Iraq: "God told me to strike at al Qaeda and I struck them, and then he instructed me to strike at Saddam [Hussein], which I did."[131]

Of course, collective crusades are fed equally from both sides. In talking about 9/11 in a *Time* magazine "Profile," Osama bin Laden said: "In today's wars, there are no morals. We believe the worst thieves in the world today and the worst terrorists are the Americans. *We do not have to differentiate between military or civilian. As far as we are concerned, they are all targets* [my emphasis]." He added further in especially graphic terms: "The pieces of the bodies of infidels were flying like dust particles. If you would have seen it with your own eyes, you would have been very pleased, and your heart would have been filled with joy."[132] And Saddam Hussein famously said "Allah is on our side. That is why we will beat the aggressor."[133] Of course, anything he said is more likely to have been a canny political statement than a true Shadow projection. Like the popes and kings who started the Crusades, Saddam Hussein was very aware that America was the devil for much of the Arab world and that placing himself on the side of Allah was the best way to win their support.

If we discount Saddam Hussein's self-serving comments, it is clear that both sides were at the Crusader Stage, totally unaware that any Shadow projection was going on. Neither would have understood what Mohandas Gandhi meant when he said of such attitudes: "'An eye for an eye makes the whole world blind.'"[134]

## THE SHADOW PROJECTED IN RACISM

We see the Shadow projected with equal venom in racism. For example, the White Europeans who came to the New World felt totally justified in killing the American Indians and stealing their lands because they were dealing with "savages." As early as 1492, when Columbus first encountered the Arawak Indians, he commented favorably about them in his log: "Of anything they have, if you ask them for it, they never say no; rather they invite the person to share it, and show as much love as if they were giving their hearts; and whether the thing be of value or of small price, at once they are content with whatever little thing of whatever kind may be given to them."[135] But then he added: "They would make fine servants . . . . with fifty men one could keep the whole population in subjection and make them do whatever one wanted."[136] His lack of hesitation at exploiting their innocence was hardly a sign of Columbus' personal Shadow: he was simply projecting a collective view of indigenous people as little more than animals that was typical of his day.

That attitude led the White settlers who came to America to slaughter Native Americans, which in turn led the Native Americans to slaughter the White settlers in an unending series of conflicts with each side projecting the Shadow onto the other side. Of course, since the Whites soon had more people and vastly more weaponry, it became an unequal struggle. That sad story is a great blight on America's image. And, of course, an equal blight is the history of slavery in America, which was one reason (though not the only reason) for the Civil War that almost destroyed the United States. And even with the victory of the North and the end of slavery, the Negro continued to serve as a vehicle for Shadow projections for the majority of white people in the South, as well as for many others in the rest of the country. That led to the struggle for civil rights in the United States during the 1950's and 1960's.

The Shadow can be collectively projected onto any group. Throughout history the Jews have served well as "hooks" for Shadow projections. Though Jews had lived in Spain or the territories that eventually became Spain for more than a millennia, during the 14th century, anti-Semitism became rampant in Spain, and despite some ups and downs, grew still worse in the 15th century, as Jews were pushed to convert (at least on the surface) to Christianity. But gradually hatred of those "new Christians" became as great, or even greater, than of unconverted Jews. In 1492, the same year Columbus came to America, the King and Queen of Spain ordered all Jews who wouldn't convert to Christianity to leave Spain. Approximately 100,000 were forced to leave their property behind and leave. Things weren't much better for those who stayed behind.

As awful as this was, it doesn't begin to compare with the Holocaust under Hitler's rule in Germany, *when 6 million Jews were killed!* And, of course, his genocide extended past Jews to almost anyone who didn't fit Hitler's definition of Aryan: Poles, gypsies, Soviets, homosexuals, the list goes on and on. The estimate of their deaths range from 5 million to 11 million.

The list of genocides and other atrocities fed in large part by Shadow projections goes on and on. Even when we move past the Crusade Stage on to Stage 2, the Heretic or Witch-Hunt Stage, the level of hatred stays high; e.g., think of the witch hunts in Europe in which somewhere between 40,000 and 100,000 women were killed from the late 15th to the late 16th century. Think of the despicable treatment of women Suffragettes fighting for the right to vote in England, the murder of civil rights workers in the South, the shooting of the students at Kent State. In our day, perhaps homosexuals, lesbians, and transgendered men and women have become the latest group to carry such Shadow projections.

Let's not list any more since the list is endless. Any group can be singled out for a Shadow projection. The question, of course, is how to escape from these endless Shadow projections with the deep harm they cause to both those carrying the projections and to those refusing to recognize the Shadow within. And, though it might seem paradoxical, the answer is that these collective issues must be resolved by each individual in their own lives. At some point, the tipping point, enough individuals withdraw their projections onto others and things shift in the culture, in the nation. We'll discuss how the projections are withdrawn and the Shadow integrated in the next chapter.

But for now let's consider how the Shadow projections onto Afro-Americans have been considerably withdrawn and integrated over the last sixty or so years. You can almost trace the stages of the process with the change in accepted name from Negro to Black to Afro-American. Negro means black in Spanish and derives from Latin *niger*, for black. It was the least offensive term used by everyone, including Negroes themselves. In what follows, I'll use the three terms in the periods when they apply.

We might trace the beginning to sports, with the great Joe Louis holding the heavyweight boxing crown from 1937 to 1949. He was widely popular among not only Negroes of that time, but also among White Americans, not only because of his great athletic ability, but also because of his personality and actions outside the ring. Before Joe Louis, boxing was held in disrepute as a dirty sport, often fixed. In contrast, he lived a clean, quiet life outside the ring, and in the ring never fought in a fixed fight, never stood and gloated over his opponents (as Mohammed Ali loved to do, and was able to do with applause because of the difference in times). In all later rankings of the greatest heavyweight fighters of all time, he ranks either #1 or #2 (with Mohammed Ali alternating with him depending on the poll).

Just as his career was winding to an end, another great Negro athlete appeared on the scene: Jackie Robinson, who broke the color line in baseball when he joined the Brooklyn Dodgers in 1947. He won every award a player can receive in baseball, including six straight all-star appearances, one most valuable player, six world series appearances, and one world series win, before his retirement in 1956. He was elected to the baseball Hall of Fame in 1962 and posthumously received both the Presidential Medal of Freedom and the Congressional Gold Medal. In contrast to Joe Louis, Robinson was a fiery personality who nevertheless held his temper in check when goaded to fight with bigots and instead turned that anger into results on the baseball field. Just as Joe Louis' quiet acceptance of the situation was right for his time, Jackie Robinson's fire was right for his.

Then in show business, there was Nat King Cole, who at his peak was the most popular singer since Bing Crosby, even outselling Frank Sinatra. In 1956, he broke the color line on television, becoming the first Negro to have his own television show. Unfortunately, companies refused to sponsor the show, fearing boycotts in the South. But still the line had been crossed and millions of Americans had seen a suave black man with his own TV show at a time when there were only three channels to watch.

Now that the American public had absorbed these positive images of black Americans in sports and entertainment, the time was ripe for broader social change. A small number of Negro leaders, most prominently Martin Luther King, Jr., recognized the injustice of the cultural projections and refused to accept them. But, and this is critical, rather than simply pointing to White Americans as the devil, he took his cue from Gandhi's non-violent struggle in India and stressed equality among all races. This very different reaction –

rejecting the projection, and not projecting in return – was highly disconcerting to those carrying the Shadow within them. Happily his approach became the main method used during the struggle. For example, Rosa Parks simply refused to move from the back of the bus. She didn't yell, she didn't make accusation; she simply refused to move from the back of the bus. That led to a wide boycott of the bus system in Montgomery, Alabama, then to "sit-ins" in drug stores and other stores where Blacks were not allowed to eat. And I use the word "Black" now instead of "Negro" because black Americans wanted to embrace the identity given to them from outside as their own. The time of Negroes gave way to Black Pride.

The struggle was long and difficult and not fully over yet, but the difference between 1955, when Rosa Parks refused to move, and now, is dramatic. As Blacks gradually became so integrated into the total culture that young people no longer today even think in terms of black and white, the name changed again to African Americans. This took color out of the name and stressed the racial heritage instead. Of course, there is still racism and African Americans still face hurdles Caucasians don't; nevertheless, a huge shift has taken place within a lifetime of many of us.

And now we need to turn from the collective Shadow to a more detailed examination of how projections are withdrawn and the Shadow integrated at a personal level.

*It is the world of water, where all life floats in suspension; where the realm of the sympathetic system, the soul of everything living, begins; where I am indivisibly this and that; where I experience the other in myself and the other-than-myself experiences me.*

# CHAPTER 7

# UNION: JOINING WITH THE SHADOW

If you imagine someone who is brave enough to withdraw all his projections, then you get an individual who is conscious of a pretty thick shadow. Such a man has saddled himself with new problems and conflicts. He has become a serious problem to himself, as he is now unable to say that *they* do this or that, *they* are wrong, and *they* must be fought against. He lives in the "House of the Gathering." Such a man knows whatever is wrong in the world is in himself, and if he only learns to deal with his own shadow he has done something real for the world. He has succeeded in shouldering at least an infinitesimal part of the gigantic, unsolved social problems of our day.

C. G. JUNG.[137]

## RECOGNIZING OUR OWN FACE IN OTHERS:
### HOW TO WITHDRAW PROJECTIONS

Having said so many positive things about projection in chapter 4, it's time to return to practical matters and talk of how projections can be withdrawn. While projection is one of the psyche's primary methods for forcing us to deal with unwanted facts, unless we do make an attempt to see through the projection, nothing has been accomplished. When the psyche projects the image of the beloved out onto someone and we fall in love, if we never attempt to see that person as they really are, we stay trapped in the projection until the differences are so marked that we fall out of love. Then we repeat the situation over again, seeing the same inner picture we saw the last time. No growth occurs. With the shadow, there is the additional difficulty that since the projection is normally negative, we are more likely to find a hook on someone with whom we have little if any

*The shadow loves exclamation points.*

relationship. Without being forced to engage with them, we may find our anger feeding upon itself, with the issue never resolving. In poet Robert Bly's words "the issue is not so much that we do project but how long we keep the projections out there. Projection without personal contact is dangerous."[138]

Astrologer and Jungian analyst Ellynor Barz has a succinct summary of the process of withdrawing projections which fits well with the more general sense of projection I've described in this book: "Again and again in the course of our life, it is a question of becoming conscious, and that means recognizing projections and withdrawing them or taking back what we first *had* to project to the external world in order to see it at all."[139] But there are definite stages in the withdrawal process.

Marie-Louise von Franz has defined five separate stages of integrating the shadow. Two other authors have given personal variations on von Franz's stages. Let's present each briefly, beginning with von Franz's stages:

(1) **identity** (where we see only the projection);
(2) **differentiation** (where we begin to notice a difference between object and projection);
(3) **moral evaluation** (where we are forced to confront the moral issue with which the shadow presents us);
(4) **illusion** (where we are finally able to deny the reality of the projection); and finally
(5) **reflection** (where we "reflect on how such an overpowering, extremely real, and awesome experience could suddenly become nothing but self-deception").[140]

Robert Bly openly draws on von Franz's stages, but characteristically offers fresh insight in his presentation:

(1) "Shadow Material, well handled by trained conspirators, comes to rest outside the owner's psyche, and seems likely to remain out there somewhere;"
(2) "projection starts to rattle;"
(3) "state of mind in which the distressed person calls on the moral intelligence to repair the rattle;"
(4) "we feel the state of diminishment;"
(5) "eating the shadow." ("Eating our shadow is a very slow process. It doesn't happen once, but hundreds of times.")[141]

In the previous chapter, we looked briefly at Jungian analyst Wolfgang Giegerich's stages as they applied to collective Shadow projections. Now let's examine them as they apply to individuals. Giegerich says that the entire process of "shadow integration is the arrival of the shadow and our housing of it in ourselves as a (certainly unwanted) guest, and its coming into being as a psychological consciousness." To repeat from chapter 6, his stages are:

(1) the **Enemy or Crusade Stage** (in which the enemy is definitely outside us, different from us. This stage is characterized by fear);

(2) the **Heretic or Witch-Hunt Stage** (in which enough of the projection has been withdrawn that we now find the enemy among us. This stage is associated with condemnation);

(3) the **Turncoat or Subversive Stage** (in which the shadow "is wherever there is light, also in me." This stage is associated with cynicism);

(4) the **Mea Culpa Stage** (in which the existence of the shadow within our self is fully acknowledged. This stage is characterized by guilt);

(5) the **Hospitality Stage or the Accomplished Integration** (in which "consciousness now sees through the arrogance inherent in the stage of bad consciousness." "What emerges here is psychological consciousness." In other words, an identity at a higher level).[142]

As long as we are stuck in the first stage, we have no hope of dealing with the shadow. As Jung says: " if we are not aware that a property of the object is a projection, we cannot do anything else but be naively convinced that it really does belong to the object."[143] In practice, the best way to escape from the first stage is to watch for immoderate emotional outbursts, responses that are unreasonable in comparison with their provocation. Giegerich associates this with fear, which is true, but we most often experience it through anger, which masks the fear. When we find ourselves blowing our top, it is wise to always ask ourselves if the shadow isn't present. Most often it will be. In therapist Sue Campbell's succinct phrase: "the shadow loves exclamation points."[144] I've come to cherish those blowups because they mean that the shadow has appeared once more in my life and that means that new growth has started again. If we're willing to live with the discomfort the shadow can bring, we have a never-ending source of creativity and change.

If we develop a personal radar for the shadow as I'm suggesting, the second stage never occurs. The "rattling" Bly mentions is because the shadow projection is so pervasive that even the most self-serving of us comes to doubt the reality of the projection.

The third stage can be a trap from which it is difficult to escape. For the first time, there is a conscious conflict between the values that have served us well for so long and the challenges presented by the shadow. It is easy here to fall into the cynicism Giegerich mentions or even to yield to despair, as if the situation is unresolvable. Remember that the shadow has a purpose—it appears to awaken us to the possibility of a bigger life than we have lived to this point. It's not there to torment us, but to make us see possibilities that we ignored before. Thus when we get to this stage, where every way we turn seems to lead to a blind alley, we have to remember that there is a meaning to this suffering. We do not have to react like an animal with its foot caught in a trap, chewing off its own leg in order to be released.

In the fourth stage, we finally fully realize that all the troubles we've been projecting onto others lie within us. That almost inevitably causes us a great deal of guilt. Where before we felt a conflict between our conscious values and our unconscious desires, now we blame ourselves for those desires, as if we owned them. This reaction needs to be recognized as self-indulgent, as a sign of an enlarged ego that thinks it owns everything within the psyche. Remembering that it is the unconscious, not our conscious ego, which has brought us to this pass can be a sobering slap in the face which enables us to escape the fourth stage.

The last stage can take a long time or no time at all, depending on our attitude. Bly says that "eating our shadow is a very slow process." While that can be true, we can also swallow the whole shadow at one gulp. In the Renzai school of Zen Buddhism, there is a highly developed series of stages of spiritual development, each of which demands that the acolyte come to grips with a single Koan. For example, "what is the sound of one hand clapping?" Or "what is the face you wore before you were born?" The resolution of each Koan opens the student's eyes to a further stage of awareness. Regardless of this progression, each Koan is also potentially a window which can open a monk's eyes so fully that he (or she these days) can pass directly into the full awareness of Satori.[145] Similarly with the shadow, there are many stages of coming to know it and to become comfortable with it. But however long it takes, the final integration is immediate. One simply joins with the shadow, just as Ged did when he "reached out his hands, dropping his staff, and took hold of his shadow, of the black self that reached out to him. Light and darkness met, and joined, and were one."[146]

There is no way to fully delineate the pattern this stage takes for each of us. In fact, the last three stages are really wrapped up into a single stage, in which we move back and forth between moral uncertainty, guilt, and self-reflection. During the process, we get ever better at recognizing the appearance of the shadow. Initially we can only recognize it after we have reacted to it through projection. After a while, we can distinguish the emotions rising up inside us as the shadow and intercept them before we find ourselves behaving foolishly. As we gradually encounter the shadow in many different situations, it is as if we were surveying a vast area of land. We visit a wide variety of locations in a way which might seem haphazard, but is actually designed to minimize the time necessary to recognize the whole territory. When at last, the whole expanse is familiar to us, we are surprised to discover that we are no longer stuck in projections, that we see the world as it really is.

> The shadow is a tight passage, a narrow door, whose painful constriction no one is spared who goes down to the deep well. But one must learn to know oneself in order to know who one is. It is the world of water, where all life floats in suspension; where the realm of the sympathetic system, the soul of everything living, begins; where I am indivisibly this *and* that; where I experience the other in myself and the other-than-myself experiences me.
>
> C. G. Jung.[147]

In trying to describe what life is like after joining with the shadow, Jung is forced into poetry in the above passage in an attempt to capture that which is almost inexpressible. But while his language may be poetic, each of his points is almost literally true. Let's take each in turn.

*The shadow is indeed a tight passage, a narrow door, whose painful constriction no one is spared who goes down to the deep well.*

As we come to engage with the shadow, there is less and less room to avoid it in our life. This can seem terribly constricting after the freedom we previously had to do whatever we liked within our comfortable self-definition. Now seemingly everywhere we turn, we run into the shadow.

We are like the beautiful princess from chapter two, who could no longer eat or sleep or play without being accompanied by the little frog.

*But one must learn to know oneself in order to know who one is.*

This isn't quite as cryptic as it sounds. Until the shadow appears, we are as unconscious of our own processes as we are of the air we breathe. We simply are what we are and do what we do. When the shadow appears, in the process of confronting its values and contrasting them with our own, we are forced into self-consciousness. Eventually that self-consciousness leads to self-reflection and psychological change. With respect to this, Jungian analyst and Ericksonian hypnotherapist Ernest Lawrence Rossi argues that: "Self-consciousness is actually a new dimension of awareness that sets the stage for self-reflection and the possibility of changing in a self-directed way."[148] Engaging with the shadow thus necessarily involves us in the process of redefining who we are and what we believe. We will discuss this at some length in the next section of this chapter.

*It is the world of water, where all life floats in suspension; where the realm of the sympathetic system, the soul of everything living, begins.*

I find this one of Jung's most fascinating comments. After we successfully pass the shadow, life becomes fluid to an extent that it never was before. Values are no longer cast in stone; we've come to realize that nothing is what it seems, that until we personally engage with any value, it no longer has any personal existence for us. The autonomic nervous system of the body controls our heart, stomach, and other internal organs. It is composed of the parasympathetic system, which slows things down, and the sympathetic system, which speeds them up in order to respond to stress. This is where the "fight or flight" response takes place. Jung is implying that, by successfully integrating the shadow into our personality, we actually change the autonomic nervous system. (Actually we change the cortical organization of the brain, which changes how the autonomic nervous system responds, but more on this later.)

Unless we did make a permanent physiological change, we would still find our self rising to the bait every time something triggered a shadow reaction in us. By engaging with the shadow, we have gradually interposed consciousness into previously unconscious processes of the body. After integration, these become largely unconscious again, but we are able to turn our consciousness to these processes whenever we choose.

> *Where I am indivisibly this and that; where I experience the other in myself and the other-than-myself experiences me.*

Here Jung is forced to use paradox to try to capture life after passing through the challenge of the shadow. Before the shadow appears, we regard ourselves as totally separate from those around us. Once we come to realize that we experience the world through a haze of projections, we know at a visceral level that we are "indivisibly this and that." We do "experience the other in myself" and perhaps even more importantly "the other-than-myself experiences me."

### PSYCHOSYNTHESIS: HOW WE CHANGE THE BRAIN

*Growth is usually achieved through a process of struggle: basically a struggle to get free from the grip of the older conventional viewpoint so we can try new ways of living and experiencing. In experimenting with new ways of living and feeling we are actually creating new states of being.[149]*

In his seminal book, *Dreams and the Growth of Personality*, Rossi combines Jungian psychology with state-of-the-art research results, in order to develop a model of psychological change, through a process he terms *psychosynthesis*.[150] Psychosynthesis assumes that:

> any aspect of phenomenal experience (e.g., an emotion, a cognitive preoccupation, a developmental block, personality characteristics, etc.) that can be visualized and engaged in an imaginative drama may be changed thereby.[151]

As we discussed in chapter four, we live in an "unlabeled world" (to use Gerald Edelman's phrase). We come into that world with pre-existing brain structures (archetypes) that may be highly specific (as with bird songs, for example), but which still have to take their final form from our experiences with the physical world. The brain has to have mechanisms available to modify its own structure in order to improve the match between the model it carries inside and the world outside. That is, we have to learn from experience and add that knowledge to our long-term memory.

It is just within the last few years that we have actually discovered how this process takes place. When we "visualize and engage in an imaginative drama", the whole body responds, whether we are doing this in an actual real-life event, a dream, or an active imagination. The autonomic nervous system activates, making our heart beat faster and sending hormones to our body to prepare it for action. But we also send information to the brain in order to make permanent changes, if necessary, to its model of reality. Some researchers now believe that whenever the sympathetic system comes into play, *intermediate-early genes (IEGs)* are triggered. Through a process of genes creating proteins which in turn affects neural structures, these genes actually make permanent changes in the brain.[152] With changes in neural structure in place, then the cycle completes as "mind modulates the biochemical functions within the cells of all the major organ systems and tissues of the body via the autonomic nervous system."[153] In other words, the body changes the mind, then the mind changes the body. Both Jung's poetic model and Dr. Rossi's mechanism of psychosynthesis are correct.

The process of assimilating the shadow into our personality to form an expanded personality is an example par excellence of how psychosynthesis works. In earlier chapters, we have discussed three different ways in which the shadow "can be visualized and engaged in an imaginative drama": (1) through its appearance in our dreams; (2) through active imagination; (3) through its projection onto people in the outer world. The process of assimilating the shadow is identical, regardless of whether we are encountering it in dreams, active imagination, or projection. This is because, as Dr. Rossi argues:

> Every access is a reframe. Each time we access the state-dependent memory, learning and behavior processes that encode a problem, we have an opportunity to "reassociate and reorganize" or reframe that problem in a manner that resolves it .... Memory is always a constructive process whereby we actually synthesize a new subjective experience every time we recall a past event.[154]

In chapter four, we discussed the stages through which we progress as we integrate the shadow's projections, as originally developed by Marie-Louise von Franz and interpreted by Robert Bly and Wolfgang Giegerich. Let's briefly recall that process.

When the shadow first appears, we are totally trapped in the projections and have no idea that we are actually encountering our own inner issues. As we gradually become aware that our projections don't match reality, we begin to differentiate what is us from what is actually in the outer world. That split between that which

*Often, people will "twin" in dreams shortly before
they emerge into consciousness.*

we previously thought to be true and that which we are now discovering to actually be true creates a dilemma, which leads to a moral struggle. Eventually we are able to fully see through the illusion, then reflect on why it occurred. By the end of the process, we have reached a rapprochement with the shadow such that a new identity has emerged which combines who we are with the traits we needed that were hidden within the shadow.

Similarly Dr. Rossi assumes that we assimilate new material into the psyche through a process of increasing self-reflection. He carefully delineates a seven-stage model of psychosynthesis through the growth in the degree of self-reflection, as presented in our dreams. In his experimental work, psychologist Dr. Alan Moffitt further broke down Dr. Rossi's final stage into three stages, yielding a nine-stage categorization of self-reflectiveness in dreams, which follows[155]:

(1) Dreamer not in dream; objects unfamiliar; no people present

(2) Dreamer not in dream; familiar people or objects present

(3) Dreamer completely involved in dream drama; no other perspective

(4) Dreamer present predominantly as an observer

(5) Dreamer thinks over an idea or has definite communication with someone

(6) Dreamer undergoes a transformation of body, role, age, emotion, etc.

(7) Dreamer has multiple levels of awareness; simultaneously participates and observes; notices oddities while dreaming; experiences dream within a dream

(8) Dreamer has significant control in, or control over, dream story; can wake up deliberately

(9) Dreamer can consciously reflect on the fact that he/she is dreaming; lucid dreaming[156]

Over the last two decades, Dr. Moffitt has used this scale to categorize the dreams of dream subjects in his dream laboratory at Carleton University in Ottawa, Canada. He coupled this categorization with a digitized record of the EEG patterns of the subject while they were having the dream. Because the EEG patterns were stored numerically rather than graphically, he could write a program to analyze the stage of sleep in which the dream took place. The results were then stored in a minicomputer (which was cutting edge technology when he first began the project). Moffitt could then readily determine how often dreams occurred at each stage of self-reflectiveness and correlate them with the stages of sleep.

In chapter one, we mentioned one major result of this research: *instead of dreaming only occurring during REM-sleep, as has been traditionally believed, dreaming occurs during all stages of sleep.* We dream continuously through the night. Because the characteristics of the various stages of sleep are so markedly different, yet we dream in all of them, Dr. Moffitt thinks it is highly likely that we are also dreaming continuously during our waking hours. Dreaming is the process through which we assimilate new knowledge into our personality. Jung had already speculated that this was true, but Dr. Moffitt's research comes close to proving it.

If we actually assimilate knowledge the way Dr. Rossi has suggested, we would expect that all of his stages would occur at one time or another in our dreams. Most of our dreams should be ones where we are present, either silent or communicating with someone else. Much less common should be dreams where we are not even present—one end of the self-reflectiveness scale—or are so self-reflective that we are transforming, twinning, have multiple levels of awareness, etc, at the other end of the scale. In fact, Dr. Moffitt did discover that all of Dr. Rossi's stages did occur in dreams, with stages 3 and 5 the most common (i.e., where the dreamer is present in the dream) and with frequency trailing off toward the two ends of the scale.[157]

One of Dr. Moffitt's then-students, Dr. Janet Mullington, extended this research to study whether similar stages of self-reflection took place during waking hours. They did.[158] So we are dreaming all the time, day and night, and at one time or the other, our dreams fall into all the stages of self-reflection predicted by Dr. Rossi's theory. This immensely important theoretical and experimental work is still too little known.

PREPARATION FOR TRANSFORMATION:
LATE SHADOW DREAMS

*We dream a world into being that dreams us into being.*

Richard Grossinger.[159]

It is this strange duality of experience represented by the later stages of the Rossi/Moffitt scale that tells us that we are beginning to join with the shadow. Our dreams will usually acknowledge this ambiguity of identity in several ways. Often, people will "twin" in dreams shortly before they emerge into full consciousness. Transformations from one state of being to another or from one identity to another are common. Such dreams invariably mean that something new is coming into consciousness and occur most frequently at critical points in our development, such as when the shadow is merging with consciousness. Let's look at some actual late shadow dreams to see how they demonstrate this increase in self-reflection preparatory to transformation. I'll begin with a short one of my own.

### GHOST DREAM

*I am starting to become part-ghost as well as part-human. I am also just starting to be able to see what the ghost part of other people looks like.*

A ghost is a spirit, a nonmaterial identity that survives death. Perhaps we might say it is the soul, if we don't restrict that to the modern Christian view of the soul.[160] In the dream, my identity is starting to get mixed up with this ghost identity. In other words, my normal personality is becoming merged with this deeper personality. And somehow this enables me to see that deeper part—the ghost—in others.

I had this dream at a time when I had been working with patients for about a year-and-a-half, both in a halfway home for deeply disturbed young adult patients and in an outpatient clinic where patients presented less severe emotional problems. Especially in working with the former, I found myself having to come from very deep places within myself in order to help them at all. For example, I frequently worked with hypnosis and other altered states of consciousness. I would most commonly match the patient's breathing and movements until we were synchronized, then gradually slow my own breathing and movements until I had induced an altered state of consciousness in both of us. At that point, I would often feel their emotions flow through me. I cried a lot of my patients' tears; invariably that would free them up as if they had cried the tears themselves.

As I progressed with this technique, I grew increasingly better at separating their emotions from my own. It's a strange sensation at first to feel an emotion and know that it's not your own. Eventually, I found that I could go through this process at a more refined level. By this time, I no longer had to experience the patient's emotion directly. I could just stay centered, direct my attention to the patient, and then somehow I became aware of things that had to do with the patient.

Gradually, I found that I had deep knowledge of not only my psychotic patients, but also my less disturbed patients, and eventually everyone I came into contact with in the course of my life. This dream marked a point where this was still a startling experience rather than the commonplace one it later became.

## BECOMING ONE WITH THE MAGICIAN

Here is a wonderful dream where transformations are starting to take place, and the dreamer is just about ready to merge with the shadow.

The dreamer is sitting near the back of a huge auditorium. The show was nearly over and there was a good feeling in the air. A young man got up from the audience and went down the center aisle and up onto the stage. The dreamer realized the young man was a magician and a close friend. The magician took a newspaper and draped it in front of himself. Gradually a shape, which could be seen to be a vase, formed inside the newspaper. The audience gasped, then gasped more as the shape changed, becoming taller or shorter, bulging here or there, at the mere wave of the magician's hands. He finally took the newspaper away and a multi-colored vase was revealed. As he walked further toward the back of the stage, the vase continued to change beneath his hands.

As this was going on, the dreamer found himself located closer and closer to the magician. He felt that they were somehow in on this together. Finally the magician laid the vase on an altar at the back of the stag, and turned to the audience with a shrug, as if to say "that's the best I can do." The audience loved it. As the dream ended, the dreamer and the magician were touching hands, bowing to the audience.

As we discussed in chapter one, the shadow gradually changes its appearance in dreams, from the repulsive in early dreams to the familiar but scorned to a close and respected friend by late dreams. Since the dreamer regards the magician—i.e., the shadow—as a close friend, this dream clearly represents a period when the shadow is very close to being integrated into the personality. The setting is dramatic: the show is nearly over when the magician emerges unexpectedly from the audience. In other words, just as things are nearly over, the real show begins.

The magician is able to make a vase appear and transform, first hidden behind the newspaper, then eventually out in the open. A vase is a container, something that gives shape to any liquid contained within it. During our dealings with the shadow, many strange new feelings emerge inside us. At first, these new emotions are vague and unformed, which makes us feel uncomfortable. Gradually we develop new containers for those emotions, we give them new form. The containers we develop get taller or shorter, narrow or bulge, as we find the right shape to hold this new us.

At the beginning of the dream, the dreamer is at the back of the audience, strictly an observer. As the dream progresses, he comes closer and closer to the magician, until, near the end, he realizes that they are performing the magic together. At the very end of the dream, with the magic completed, they are actually touching hands. Note that by this time, the vase that was produced has been put on an altar; i.e., this new container is holy, sacred. As might be expected, this dream shortly preceded a major life change for the dreamer.

BORDER CROSSING, RITUAL, DEATH & TRANSFORMATION

Here is a dream which passes through three separate stages which we might call: (1) border crossing; (2) ritual; and (3) death and transformation.

**Border Crossing:** the dreamer took a trip with a lady friend across the border into Mexico City. After they checked in, showed their passports, etc., the woman became a man, then eventually the dreamer's brother. The dreamer argues with the desk clerk.

**Ritual:** Still in Mexico City, the dreamer, his brother, and his father went into a Catholic Church for some non-religious purpose. A service was going on, however, so they knelt in pews at the back of the church. The priest, probably a bishop, was very old. His great-grandson, who was also a priest, was helping with the ceremony. A woman came along tucking napkins under people's chins to prepare for communion. This irritated the dreamer, who yanked off the napkin.

**Death and Transformation:** After the service, the dreamer, his father, and brother came out of the church. The dreamer said he wanted to be alone in his own car. As he sat there at the foot of a hill, a man in another car came driving down the hill straight toward him. The dreamer remained irritated, but not fearful. When the two cars crashed, the dreamer felt that things just disappeared, as if the old went out of existence and something new came into existence.

Transformations of the personality, psychosynthesis in Dr. Rossi's phrase, take place on the border between conscious and unconscious. We will see this again in the dream that follows. In the above dream, the dreamer crosses over the border between the United States and Mexico. When he does, he is not only in a foreign country, he is immediately in its capital, Mexico City. Identities are less defined now that he has crossed over into the unconscious: his female companion changes first into a male friend, then into his brother. Later still, his father appears, without any explanation in the dream.

From the time he crosses over into the unconscious, the dreamer is irritable and argumentative. This irritability is a common experience when the boundaries between conscious and unconscious, ego and shadow, are beginning to dissolve. Normally in our dreams, we are unaware of this distinction (i.e., during the Rossi/Moffitt stages 3 or 5), and just accept the dream world without question. When we get to the later stages, where the degree of self-reflection increases, the conflict between conscious and unconscious values makes us itchy and uncomfortable.

The dreamer, who had been raised Catholic, goes to a Catholic Church. Though he thinks it's for nonreligous reasons, he is nevertheless forced to sit through a church service. Jung often said that all emotional problems in the second half of life are at the deepest level spiritual problems, attempts to find the meaning in life. This service is conducted by a combination of the very old and the very young, the bishop and his great-grandson. This combination appears so often that it has been identified in Jungian psychology as the "Puer/Senex" problem; i.e., the need to reconcile the traditional wisdom represented by the old ("Senex"), with the need for novelty and change, represented by the young ("Puer"). While we are trapped in this dilemma, we can flip-flop between unthinking acquiescence to conventional values and angry rebellion against those same values. In the dream, this process is quite advanced, as age and youth are already working in harmony to conduct the proper spiritual ritual, though the dreamer is not yet comfortable with the results.

Even with the ritual concluded, the dreamer remains irritable. But now the denouement is at hand. He separates from his father and brother in order for the ego to face its own death. When the car crash occurs, the dreamer is finally aware that a major change has taken place with the old replaced by the new. Of course, he has no idea what that means yet. And there is no picture in the dream of what the transformed dreamer looks like. In other words, this is still an incomplete transformation that has to precede by some time the actual merging of ego and shadow.

### Ego & Shadow Merge

A dream where we actually see the ego personality merge with the shadow follows.[161]

> A man—who was sometimes the dreamer—was inside a long rectangular building, looking out the window in back at the beach behind them. There was a man wading at the edge of the beach. The dreamer opened the window, jumped through it, and ran across the beach toward the wader. A guard inside yelled at him to stop, while another man, who the dreamer thought of as the "spy," also ran across the beach toward the swimmer. When the spy reached the swimmer, there was a struggle, and they both went under. When the wader came up alone, it appeared that the spy had drowned, but the dreamer was aware that it was actually the wader who had drowned. At that point, the spy became the dreamer.
>
> After this transformation, the dreamer swam out further. The ocean had now been transformed into a big swimming pool. A beautiful woman swam into his arms and they kissed passionately.

There is an ambiguity of identity at the beginning of the dream: the dreamer is observing the dream, yet he is also in some way the man in the building, who is in turn also an observer. So clearly the dreamer is dealing with material that he is both experiencing and reflecting on at the same time.

Two other males figure heavily in the dream: the wader at the edge of the beach and the spy. The unconscious is frequently represented in our dreams by the ocean, which is the source of all physical life, just as the unconscious is the source of all psychic life. The edge of the beach is again that border territory, discussed in the previous dream, where conscious and unconscious merge. Note that in this dream, the one male figure is wading right at that border point. This could have been an early shadow dream where the dreamer was just starting to interact with the unconscious. In fact, it is a late shadow dream where transformation is about to take place at the border between conscious and unconscious.

A spy is someone who presents a false identity, in order to infiltrate an organization and obtain secret information. When we are gathering information from the unconscious that is exactly how our position feels. We don't quite approve of what we're doing; it feels somewhat criminal, yet we do it anyway because we need the knowledge. It takes a long time to become comfortable with our role as a spy. A true spy is a professional who no longer struggles with any moral dilemma over his actions.

This dream presents the integration of the shadow into the dreamer in the most dramatic fashion possible. There is a struggle between the man who merely wades at the edge of the water there and the spy. In other words, a struggle between that part of us which thinks we can be casual about this process, that it won't truly affect our life, and that part which is a professional, ready to do what must be done. In the struggle, their separate identities become confused so that it appears that the spy has drowned in the unconscious while actually it is the wader who has drowned. At that realization, the dreamer becomes the spy. This is a complex merging of three separate aspects of the personality into a new unified personality that incorporates all three.

The postscript tells us a little about what happens when we complete the shadow process. First, what seemed to us an unlimited expanse of ocean is now merely a big swimming pool. This is because most of our struggle with the shadow is a struggle with the personal unconscious; i.e., with those personal traits that we have either denied or not developed. The shadow itself is archetypal and beyond our personal limits, but our encounter with it is largely with our own issues. Second, "a beautiful woman swims into the dreamer's arms and they kiss passionately." When we have finally integrated the shadow, the darkness we have struggled with goes away. The world becomes suddenly very attractive, and our life is once more filled with passion.

Just as Ged finally found peace with his shadow, and Gollum was able to bring Frodo's ring quest to a successful end, we have reached the end of the journey we have taken with the shadow. It's been a wonderful companion along the way and I hope, has become an honored guest in your life. To close, I'd like to tell a Sufi story about a man who was so virtuous that angels offered to give him any gift he desired: the gift of miracles, of healing hands, etc. He asked only to be able to make the world better without anyone, including himself, being aware that he was responsible. So the angels decided that whenever his shadow was behind him, where he could not see it, it would heal and console and bring joy.

> Wherever he walked, his shadow caused dried rivers to flow, withered plants to flower, and brought gladness to the hearts of men, women, and children. The saint simply went about his life, and all this happened in his wake. After a time, his name was forgotten, and he was simply called the "Holy Shadow."[162]

Can there be a more beautiful example of what it means to oneself and the world to integrate the Shadow.

# AFTERWORD:
# THE INTERPLAY OF LIGHT AND DARK

The early hours of the morning
Lift the shadow of self-deception
from the world.
The Darkness of the night
Reveals what the light of day
—cannot
For the glare of the light
Confuses and softens the
harsh realities of the soul
That only Darkness in its
all enveloping presence can reveal.

KATHERINE ROBERTSON.

Before I was asked to write this book, I had already written about the shadow in several books and didn't think that I had much left to say about it. In the course of writing this book, I found that I was wrong. For one thing, perhaps more than any other writer on the shadow, I believe in the inherent good of the shadow, its attempt to make us become the person we were intended to be. The shadow is a paradox. While it initially appears to us as loathsome and despicable, it actually contains all our future potentialities for development. I have always tried to welcome the shadow into my life when it makes an appearance in my dreams. Perhaps because of my welcome, the shadow has always been good to me.

I originally came to Jungian psychology when I experienced an identity crisis during my mid-30s, which I have described briefly in chapter one. After struggling on my own with the issues for some months, I went into a Jungian analysis. In the first session, my analyst told me that we would be working a great deal with my dreams. When I told him that I never dreamed, he asked me to make an attempt to record any that I did have. I went home and before going to sleep, I put a pencil and notebook by my bed. That night I had five dreams! For approximately the next twenty years, I recorded an average of three dreams a night. In more recent years, I haven't needed to record more than occasional dreams.

As I began to actively record and work with my dreams, I also began reading Jung. He was as much of a revelation as the dreams. The combination of the strange new landscape of dreams, with Dr. Jung's expanded view of the possibilities of human development, was like stepping into a new world for me. I've never left that world since.

Most of my work over that first year turned out to be shadow work. Though I experienced a great deal of depression during that year (and in the years since as everyone does who deals with the unconscious), there was also a great deal of exhilaration. I had a sense that I was doing something important, not only for myself, but for some deeper power within me. Since the shadow was where I was doing my work, I honored the shadow. And it honored me in turn.

After a little under a year, I attended a series of introductory lectures on Jungian psychology held at the local Jung Institute. At the first lecture, the speaker, who was very good otherwise, presented the shadow largely as the dark, evil side of our personality to which we have to become in some way reconciled. I raised my hand and gently told of how the shadow contains everything that we can ever be, of how the shadow is thus our first look at the Self, that part of us that comes closest to divinity. I felt good that I managed to get the point across and did so in a way that didn't insult the speaker. Afterwards, as I was walking out, a woman approached me and introduced herself as the then-president of the institute. She thanked me for what I had said about the shadow as she would otherwise have had to interrupt herself and that might have embarrassed the speaker. It was my first indication that perhaps I understood the shadow better than most. The woman became one of my closest friends.

Several years later, at a time when I was doing my training as a counselor at a local out-patient clinic, I attended a weekend conference held for all the counselors and supervisors (i.e., licensed psychologists who helped the counselors learn their trade through weekly supervisory groups). During the afternoon, I sat in on a workshop my supervisor was giving on the shadow. He wasn't Jungian and was coming to this material for the first time himself. He presented the shadow as the "dark force" from "Star Wars," which made me cringe. When the audience started asking him tough questions, I managed to find a way to help him with much the same sort of presentation I had made at the introductory Jungian series. He was very grateful and afterwards we went off together and talked for quite a while about the shadow.

Over the years, I've found again and again that most people have a hard time viewing the shadow as anything other than their evil side. Freud had much the same view of the unconscious, the id, viewing it solely as our primitive needs and desires which will always be at odds with our civilized rationality. As long as we have this simplistic view, our attempts to integrate the shadow are doomed, at best, to a tension-filled truce. Throughout most of our lives, we have seen just such an attitude projected out onto those who we regard as our enemies, such as the Soviet Union through the post-WWII era.

Though I in no way intend to denigrate traditional religious views, they frequently contribute to the problem. Christianity and Judaism, for example, present morality in terms of right and wrong, good and evil. Virtue is rewarded, vice punished. Our goal is to seek the light and cast off the darkness. Unfortunately, life is more complex. Good and evil, virtue and vice, are not always so readily separated. And darkness may simply be the unknown, where light has never had an opportunity to shine.

Anyone who isn't a Pollyanna knows that there is evil in the world. Yet it does no good at all for us to equate the shadow with that evil. The shadow is in many ways beyond good and evil—simply a natural force like the wind and the tides.

### But even that doesn't do it justice.

As we come to know the shadow and to integrate it into our lives, we become better people, not worse. We are more tolerant, more capable of putting ourselves in the place of another. We see more possibilities in any situation than are presented in any simplistic scheme of morality.

### But even that doesn't honor it enough.

People who have integrated the shadow into their personality normally become genuinely kind people. They think about others and care for their welfare in a way that is still uncommon. They practice the religious virtues not out of fear of the consequences, but simply because they care about other people. In M. Esther Harding's words: "by the acceptance of the black substance which adheres to the shadow, we should have taken the first step in the individuation process and in the development of a true self-consciousness."[163]

If there is anything I hope you gain from this book, it is the simple realization that life is not out to get you and that the shadow is your guide to a better life.

*If there is anything I hope you gain from this book, it is the*
*simple realization that life is not out to get you and that*

**the shadow is your guide to a better life.**

# ENDNOTES

1. Wilhelm Reich, *Character Analysis*, 3rd edition (New York, Simon and Schuster, Touchstone, 1972). Also see Ken Dychtwald, *Body-Mind* (New York: Jove Books, 1977), for summary and updated information on Reich's ideas.

2. Gail Sheehy, *Passages* (New York, Bantam Books, 1977).

3. A. I. Allenby describing a conversation with C. G. Jung, in *C. G. Jung Speaking: Interviews and Encounters*, William McGuire and R. F. C. Hull, editors (Princeton: Princeton University Press, Bollingen Series, 1977), p. 158.

4. William Blake, "The Marriage of Heaven and Hell", in Northrop Frye, Ed., *Selected Poetry and Prose of William Blake* (New York: Modern Library, 1953), p. 125.

5. Ursula Le Guin, *A Wizard of Earthsea* (New York: Bantam Books, 1968).

6. Throughout this book, my personal comments are indented and in italics. I've also indented and Italicized dreams. In a few cases, where things might get confused, such as my discussion of Jacob's struggle with the mysterious stranger in chapter two, I've used clearly contrasting type formats.

7. Quotation from Ursula Le Guin, *A Wizard of Earthsea*, p. 179.

8. 1 Corinthians 13:11

9. Charles Mills Gayley, *The Classic Myths in English Literature, 2nd edition* (Boston: Ginn & Company, 1894), p. 45.

10. Yousuf Karsh, in *Parade*, Dec. 3, 1978.

11. M. Esther Harding, *The I and the not-I: A Study in the Development of Consciousness* (Princeton: Princeton University Press, Bollingen Series LXXIX, 1965), p. 90.

12. ibid, p. 94.

13. C. G. Jung, "The Tavistock Lectures, *Collected Works, Vol. 18: The Symbolic Life* (Princeton: Princeton University Press, Bollingen Series, 1969), ¶ 11.

14. See C. G. Jung, *Collected Works, Vol. 8: The Structure and Dynamics of the Psyche, 2nd Edition* (Princeton: Princeton University Press, Bollingen Series, 1969), ¶ 397. For an earlier such speculation, see William James, *The Varieties of Religious Experience* (New York, 1902), pp. 226-7.

15. Carl Sagan, *The Dragons of Eden* (New York: Ballantine Books), 1977.

16. both quotes in Carl Sagan, *The Dragons of Eden*, p. 57.

17. "Gray's Theory Incorporates Earlier Evolutionary Model of 'Triune Brain,'" *Brain/Mind Bulletin* (March 29, 1982), p. 4.

18. Konrad Z. Lorenz, *King Solomon's Ring* (New York: Harper Torchbooks, Harper & Row, 1952), p. 140.

19. Actually even the image isn't actually stored. It's rather that the brain is able to access the archetypal information and process it either as behavior or as an intermediate image, which can allow more complex behavior to take place.

20. These modern views of memory and sense perception as constructivist in nature are spread over a variety of disciplines at present; the implications are still in the process of being worked out.

21. C. G. Jung, *Collected Works, Volume 7: Two Essays on Analytical Psychology, 2nd Edition*, (Princeton: Princeton University Press, Bollingen Series, 1966), ¶ 78.

22. C. G. Jung, *Modern Man in Search of a Soul* (New York: Harvest Book, Harcourt, Brace & World, Inc., 1933), p. 104. This was the first book I ever read by Jung.

23. Gail Sheehy, *Passages: Predictable Crises of Adult Life* (New York: Ballantine Books, 2006), p. xvi.

24. C. G. Jung. *Wandlunger und Symbole der Libido* (original version) (Leipzig and Vienna, 1912), p. 221.

25. William Blake, "The Marriage of Heaven and Hell", in Northrop Frye, Ed., *Selected Poetry and Prose of William Blake* (New York: Modern Library, 1953), p. 125.

26. I have also previously told this story in *After the End of Time* (Virginia Beach: Inner Vision, 1990), pp. 171-2.

27. C. G. Jung, "The Tavistock Lectures, ¶ 40.

28. Marie-Louise von Franz, *Projection and Re-Collection in Jungian Psychology* (La Salle & London: Open Court, 1980), p.3.

29. C. G. Jung, *Collected Works, Volume 5: Symbols of Transformation, 2nd edition* (Princeton: Princeton University Press, Bollingen Series XX, 1967), ¶ 581.

30. All quotes from C. G. Jung, *Modern Man in Search of a Soul*, p. 105.

31. C. G. Jung, *Collected Works, Vol. 14: Mysterium Coniunctionis, 2nd edition* (Princeton: Princeton University Press, Bollingen Series, 1963/1970), ¶ 470.

32. Richard Grossinger, "The Dream Work", in *Dreams are Wiser than Men*, Richard Russo, editor (Berkeley: North Atlantic Books, 1987), p. 205.

33. See Alan Moffitt, "The Creation of Self in Dreaming and Waking", *Psychological Perspectives*, Issue 30 (Los Angeles: C. G. Jung Institute, 1994), pp. 42-69.

34. J. R. R. Tolkein, *The Hobbit* (Boston: Houghton Mifflin Company, 1966).

35. Composed of three volumes: *The Fellowship of the Ring*, *The Two Towers*, and *The Return of the King*. All by J. R. R. Tolkein, in the 1965 Ballantine P.B. edition.

36. Dream contributed by Edward Harper to on-line discussion on the Shadow, "Jung Book Talks", *CSF Seminars On Line*, 1/27/97-2/2/97.

37. Julius C. Travis, "The Hierarchy of Symbols", in *The Shaman From Elko: Papers In Honor of Joseph L. Henderson*, Garth Hill, editor (Boston: SIGO Press, 1978), p. 225.

38. Edward F. Edinger, *The Mysterium Lectures* (Toronto: Inner City Books, 1995), pp. 88-89.

39. Jack Zipes, Translator, *The Complete Fairy Tales of the Brothers Grimm* (New York: Bantam Books, P.B. edition, 1992), pp. 2-5.

40. Richard Grossinger, "The Dream Work", in *Dreams are Wiser than Men*, Richard Russo, editor (Berkeley: North Atlantic Books, 1987), p. 204.

41. Kathleen Jenks, *Journey of a Dream Animal* (New York: The Julian Press, 1975), p. 23.

42. M. Esther Harding, *The "I" and the "Not-I"*, p. 16.

43. Both quotations from story in M. Esther Harding, *The "I" and the "Not-I"* (Princeton: Princeton University Press, Bollingen Series,1965), p. 84.

44. C. G. Jung, "On the Nature of the Psyche" (1947/1954), *Collected Works, Vol. 8: The Structure and Dynamics of the Psyche, 2nd edition* (Princeton: Princeton University Press, Bollingen Series, 1969), ¶ 385.

45. C. G. Jung, "The Transcendent Function" (1916), *Collected Works, Vol. 8: The Structure and Dynamics of the Psyche, 2nd edition* (Princeton: Princeton University Press, Bollingen Series, 1969), ¶ 137.

46. C. G. Jung, "Analytical Psychology and Weltanschauung" (1927), *Collected Works, Vol. 8: The Structure and Dynamics of the Psyche, 2nd edition* (Princeton: Princeton University Press, Bollingen Series, 1969), ¶ 695.

47. See Robin Robertson, *Beginner's Guide to Jungian Psychology* (York Beach Main: Nicolas-Hays, Inc, 1992) for a full treatment of the archetypal figures of the Anima/Animus and Self, that appear after the Shadow.

48. Marie-Louise von Franz, *An Introduction to the Psychology of Fairy Tales* (Irving, Texas: Spring Publications, 1978), p.1.

49. Janet Dallett, "Active Imagination in Practice," in *Jungian Analysis*, Murray Stein, Editor (La Salle, Illinois: Open Court Publishing), p. 176.

50. John Talley's comments on Alfred Plaut's "An Undivided World Includes the Shadow", in *The Archetype of Shadow in a Split World: Proceedings of the Tenth International Congress for Analytical Psychology, Berlin, 1986*, Mary Ann Mattoon, editor (Einsiedeln, Switzerland: Daimon Verlag), p. 18.

51. Richard Noll, "Multiple Personality, Dissociation, and C. G. Jung's Complex Theory", *The Journal of Analytical Psychology, Vol. 34, No. 4* (October 1989), p. 364. Emphasis in original.

52. much of the material here and following on MPD, especially in relationship to Jung's views, can be found in Richard Noll's seminal paper "Multiple Personality, Dissociation, and C. G. Jung's Complex Theory".

53. Théodore Flournoy, *Spiritism and Psychology* (New York and London: Harper & Brothers, 1911), p. 57.

54. C. G. Jung, "The Transcendent Function" (1916), *Collected Works, Vol. 8: The Structure and Dynamics of the Psyche, 2nd edition* (Princeton: Princeton University Press, Bollingen Series, 1969), ¶ 193.

55. Robert A. Baker, *Hidden Memories* (New York: Prometheus Books, 1996), p. 88

56. both quotations by Frederick Myers, in Sonu Shamdasani, "Automatic Writing and the Discovery of the Unconscious", *Spring 54* (1993), p. 114.

57. See Alan Moffitt, "The Creation of Self in Dreaming and Waking," *Psychological Perspectives*, Issue 30 (Los Angeles: C. G. Jung Institute, 1994), pp. 42-69. For

more details of the research, see Sheila Purcell, Alan Moffitt, and Robert Hoffman, "Waking, Dreaming, and Self-Regulation", in Alan Moffitt, Milton Kramer, and Robert Hoffman (editors), *The Functions of Dreaming* (Albany: State University of New York Press, 1993), pp. 197-260.

58. Sonu Shamdasani, "Introduction: Encountering Hélène–Théodore Flournoy and the Genesis of Subliminal Psychology," in Théodore Flournoy, *From India to the Planet Mars: A Case of Multiple Personality with Imaginary Languages* (Princeton: Princeton University Press, 1994.)

59. the pseudonym of Élise-Catherine Müller (1861-1929).

60. I'm using the term channeling, since we are more familiar with channels in our time than mediums. Other than the difference in perspective between the later nineteenth century and our own time, there seems little difference between someone conducting a seance in which different voices spoke through the medium, and a modern channel who allows personalties to speak through them.

61. In this description and conclusions, I have drawn heavily on Sonu Shamdasani's wonderful new edition of Théodore Flournoy, *From India to the Planet Mars*. Also see Robert A. Baker's *Hidden Memories* (New York: Prometheus Books, 1996), chapters 2 and 3.

62. Pierre Janet, *L'Automatisme Psychologigue* (Paris: Alcan, 1889), p. 135; translated by Sonu Shamdasani, in "Automatic Writing and the Discovery of the Unconscious", p. 119.

63. See the following by Jane Roberts: *Adventures in Consciousness* (New York: Bantam, 1975); *Psychic Politics* (Englewood Cliffs, New Jersey: Prentice-Hall, 1976); *The God of Jane: A Psychic Manifesto* (New York: Prentice Hall Press, 1981).

64. Paul Hawken, *The Magic of Findhorn* (New York: Harper & Row, 1975).

65. Quotation in Sonu Shamdasani, "Automatic Writing and the Discovery of the Unconscious", p. 118.

66. For an excellent, even-handed study of channeling, see Arthur Hastings, *With the Tongues of Men and Angels* (Fort Worth: Holt, Rinehart and Winston, 1991).

67. "Active Imagination", unpublished record of a talk given in Zurich on Sept. 25, 1967 at a Special Lecture Series for the C. G. Jung Educational Center of Houston, Texas, p. 7.

68. C. G. Jung, *Collected Works, Vol. 14: Mysterium Coniunctionis, 2nd edition* (Princeton: Princeton University Press, Bollingen Series, 1963/1970), par. 604n. I've always tried to obey Jung's injunction and tell this story as often as possible.

69. Joan Chodorow, ed., *Jung on Active Imagination* (Princeton: Princeton University Press, 1997), p. 3.

70. The term "altered states of consciousness" was coined by psychologist Charles T. Tart in his seminal collection of readings of the same name: *Altered States of Consciousness* (New York, John Wiley & Sons, Inc., 1969).

71. C. G. Jung, "The technique of differentiation between the ego and the figures of the unconscious," *Collected Works*, vol. 7 (Princeton: Princeton University Press, 1953/1966; 3rd printing 1973), par.

72. not Gestalt psychology, the two are quite different.

73. For two excellent books representing the skeptic's position on altered states of conscious, see Robert A. Baker, *They Call it Hypnosis* (Buffalo, New York: Prometheus Books, 1990), and Robert A. Baker, *Hidden Memories: Voices and Visions from Within* (Amherst, New York: Prometheus Books, 1996).

74. Janet Dallett, "Active Imagination in Practice," p. 180.

75. Joan Chodorow, ed., *Jung on Active Imagination*, p. 2.

76. See Eligio Stephen Gallegos, *The Personal Totem Pole: Animal Imagery, the Chakras, and Psychotherapy* (Santa Fe, New Mexico: Blue Feather Press, 1987).

77. C. G. Jung, "The Tavistock Lectures", 1935, *Collected Works, Vol. 18: The Symbolic Life* (Princeton: Princeton University Press, Bollingen Series, 1955/1980), ¶ 94. Also C. G. Jung, "Mind and Earth", 1928/1931, *Collected Works, Vol. 10: Civilization in Transition, 2nd edition* (Princeton: Princeton University Press, Bollingen Series, 1964/1970), ¶ 94.

78. C. G. Jung, "The Transcendent Function" (1916), prefatory note between par. 130 & 131.

79. David Fideler, Notes for Manius of Samaria, *The Life of Proclus*, David Fideler, editor (Grand Rapids: Phanes Press, 1986), p. 61.

80. Richard Noll, "Multiple Personality, Dissociation, and C. G. Jung's Complex Theory", p. 365.

81. Henry Reed, Channeling Your Higher Self (Virginia Beach, VA: A.R.E. Press, 2007).

82. Henry Reed, Channeling Your Higher Self , pp. 194-5.

83. Henry Reed, Channeling Your Higher Self , p. 198.

84. Ira Progoff, The Image of an Oracle (New York: Helix Press Book, Garrett Publications, 1964).

85. Ira Progoff, The Image of an Oracle, pp. 357-8.

86. Henry Reed, Channeling Your Higher Self , p. 199.

87. Ira Progoff, The Image of an Oracle, p. 359.

88. For an excellent, even-handed study of channeling, see Arthur Hastings, With the Tongues of Men and Angels (Fort Worth: Holt, Rinehart and Winston, 1991).

89. C. G. Jung, *CW9ii: Aion*, pars. 17.

90. projection comes from the Latin *projectus*, which is the past participle of *prociere*, "to throw out".

91. Adolf Guggenbühl-Craig, *Power in the Helping Professions* (Irving, TX: Spring Publications, 1979), p. 45.

92. M. Esher Harding, *The I and the not–I*, p. 78.

93. Henry Reed, "Intimacy and Psi: Explorations in Psychic Closeness", *Journal of Analytical Psychology 41, Part1* (1986), pp. 81-116; "Close Encounters in the Liminal Zone: Experiments in Imaginal Communication", *Journal of Analytical Psychology 41, Part 2* (1986), pp.203-226 .

94. C. G. Jung, "General Aspects of Dream Psychology," *Collected Works, Vol. 8: The Structure and Dynamics of the Psyche, 2nd edition* (Princeton: Princeton University Press, Bollingen Series, 1969), ¶ 507.

95. C. G. Jung, "General Aspects of Dream Psychology," *Collected Works, Vol. 8: The Structure and Dynamics of the Psyche, 2nd edition* (Princeton: Princeton University Press, Bollingen Series, 1969), ¶ 509.

96. William James, *The Principles of Psychology, Volume One*, (Unabridged reprint of 1890 edition of Holt and Company) (New York: Dover, 1950), p. 76.

97. Gerald Durrell, *Encounters with Animals* (New York: Avon Books, 1958), pp. 62-66.

98. William Sulis, "Collective Intelligence as a Model for the Unconscious," *Psychological Perspectives, Issue 35* (Los Angeles: C. G. Jung Institute, 1997).

99. Gerald Durrell, *Encounters with Animals*, pp. 74-78.

100. William James, *Psychology (Briefer Course)* (New York: Holt, 1890), pp. 3-4.

101. for much more on the history of views of the brain and mind, see Marc Jeannerod, *The Brain Machine: the Development of Neurophysiological Thought* (Cambridge, Massachusetts and London, England: Harvard University Press, 1985).

102. Gerald M. Edelman, *Neural Darwinism*, pp. 26-7.

103. transference is the formal psychoanalytic term for the patient's projection of their issues onto the psychoanalyst. We have been discussing projection in a broader sense, of which transference is only a single example.

104. Edward T. Hall, *Beyond Culture* (Garden City, New York: Anchor Books, 1977), pp. 25-40.

105. Herbert Weiner, *9½ Mystics: the Kabbala Today* (New York, Chicago, San Francisco: Holt, Rinehart, and Winston, 1969), p. 7.

106. Saint Augustine in his *Enchiridion*, quotation in Anthony S. Mercatante, *Good and Evil in Myth & Legend* (New York: Barnes & Noble, 1978), p. 7.

107. Saint Thomas Aquinas, quotation in Anthony S. Mercatante, *Good and Evil in Myth & Legend*, p. 8.

108. See Robin Robertson, *Beginner's Guide to Jungian Psychology* (York Beach Main: Nicolas-Hays, Inc, 1982) for a full treatment of Jung's model of psychological types.

109. C. G. Jung, *Collected Works, Volume 9ii: Aion: Researches into the Phenomenology of the Self, 2nd Edition* (Princeton: Princeton University Press, Bollingen Series XX, 1959), p. 10.

110. Jean Piaget, *The Moral Judgement of the Child* (New York: Free Press, 1965).

111. Kenneth Gergen, et al (editors), *Social Psychology: Explorations in Understanding* (New York: Random House, 1974), p. 69.

112. Sara Sanborn, "Means and Ends: Moral Development and Moral Education", in *Annual Editions: Readings in Psychology '74/'75* (Guilford, Connecticut: Dushkin Publishing Group, 1974), p. 167.

113. Lawrence Kohlberg, "Stage and Sequence: The Cognitive-Developmental Approach to Socialization," in D. A. Goslin (ed.), *Handbook of Socialization Theory and Research* (Chicago: Rand McNally, 1969), p.379.

114. See Kenneth Gergen, et al (editors), *Social Psychology: Explorations in Understanding*, pp. 69-72.

115. J. R. Tolkein, *The Fellowship of the Ring* (New York: Ballantine Books, 1965), p. vii.

116. J. R. Tolkein, *The Return of the King* (New York: Ballantine Books, 1965), p. 263.

117. J. R. Tolkein, *The Return of the King*, p. 263.

118. J. R. Tolkein, *The Return of the King*, p. 268.

119. J. R. Tolkein, *The Return of the King*, p. 274.

120. J. R. Tolkein, *The Return of the King*, p. 277.

121. C. G. Jung, *Memories, Dreams, Reflections*, p. 175.

122. original German edition 1912; later revised and eventually published in its English edition as *Collected Works*, vol., 5: *Symbols of Transformation*, 2nd ed. with corrections (Princeton: Princeton University Press, Bollingen Series XX, 1967).

123. C. G. Jung, *Memories, Dreams, Reflections*, p. 176.

124. e-mail of 4/21/10.

125. Wolfgang Giegerich, "The Advent of the Guest: Shadow Integration and the Rise of Psychology", *Spring 51* (1991), pp. 86-106.

126. quote from the Nixon Library in Yorba Linda, CA. Accessed on 5/3/10 at http://www.nixonlibrary.gov/thelife/apolitician/thesenator.php.

127. Stephen Mansfield, *The Faith of George W. Bush* (Lake Mary, FL: Charisma House, 2004), p. 109.

128. "America's New War: President Bush Talks with Reporters at Pentagon", CNN.com, 17 September 2001. (URL accessed on 2007-01-24).

129. See http://georgewbush-whitehouse.archives.gov/news/releases/2001/09/2001 0916-2.html (accessed 4/24/10).

130. reported by John King on CNN, 9/27/02.

131. Palestinian Authority Prime Minister Abu Mazen quoting Bush when they met in Aqaba; reported in The Haaretz Reporter by Arnon Regular.
See http://www.gainesvillehumanists.org/dubya.htm (accessed 05/01/10)

132. "Osama Bin Laden Profile," *Time*, 9/16/01.

133. date unknown. Widely quoted on the web.

134. M. K. Gandhi, *The Story of My Life* (Ahmedabad, India: Navajivan Publishing House, 1955).

135. David E. Stannard, *American Holocaust: Columbus and the Conquest of the New World* (New York: Oxford University Press, 1992), pg.63.

136. John Cummins (trans.). *The Voyage of Christopher Columbus*, http://www.archive.org/stream/voyageofchristop005194mbp/voyageofchristop005194mbp_djvu.txt (accessed on 4/24/10).

137. C. G. Jung, *CW11: Psychology and Religion, 2nd Edition* (Princeton: Princeton University Press, Bollingen Series, 1969), par. 140.

138. Robert Bly, *A Little Book on the Human Shadow* (San Francisco, Harper & Row, 1988), p. 23.

139. Ellynor Barz, *Gods and Planets* (Wilmette, IL: Chiron Publications), 1991, p. xvi.

140. Marie-Louise von Franz, *Projection and Re-Collection in Jungian Psychology* (La Salle & London: Open Court, 1980), p. 10.

141. Robert Bly, *A Little Book on the Human Shadow* (San Francisco, Harper & Row, 1988), pp. 29-43.

142. Wolfgang Giegerich, "The Advent of the Guest: Shadow Integration and the Rise of Psychology", *Spring 51* (1991), pp. 86-106.

143. C. G. Jung, "General Aspects of Dream Psychology," *Collected Works, Vol. 8: The Structure and Dynamics of the Psyche, 2nd edition* (Princeton: Princeton University Press, Bollingen Series, 1969), par. 507.

144. contributed by Sue Campbell to on-line discussion on the Shadow, "Jung Book Talks", *CSF Seminars On Line* , 1/27/97-2/2/97.

145. See Yoel Hoffman, *The Sound of One Hand: 281 Zen Koans with Answers* (New York: Basic Books, 1975).

146. See the introduction for the prior mention of this.

147. C. G. Jung, "The Archetypes of the Collective Unconscious", *CW9i: The Archetypes and the Collective Unconscious*, par. 45.

148. Ernest Lawrence Rossi, *Dreams and the Growth of Personality, 2nd edition* (New York: Brunner/Mazel, 1972/1985), p. 13. He has since published a revised 3rd edition, retitled *Dreams, Consciousness, Spirit* (Malibu, CA: Palisades Gateway Publishing).

149. Ernest Lawrence Rossi, *Dreams and the Growth of Personality*, p. 4.

150. Dr. Rossi's use of the term "psychosynthesis" differs from that of Roberto Assagioli, who originally coined the term in the early days of the 20th century.

151. Ernest Lawrence Rossi, *Dreams and the Growth of Personality*, p. 185.

152. Ernest Lawrence Rossi, "The Psychophysiological Basis of Healing Processes: the Communication Loop Between Mind and Gene", in Wayne Jonas and Jeffrey Levin, *Textbook of Complementary and Alternative Medicine* (New York: Williams & Wilkins, upcoming 1998).

153. Ernest Lawrence Rossi, *The Psychobiology of Mind-Body Healing* (New York and London: W. W. Norton & Company, 1986), p. 108.

154. Ernest Lawrence Rossi, *The Psychobiology of Mind-Body Healing*, pp. 68-9.

155. See Alan Moffitt, "The Creation of Self in Dreaming and Waking", *Psychological Perspectives, Issue 30* (Los Angeles: C. G. Jung Institute), 1994), pp. 42-69. For more details of the research, see Sheila Purcell, Alan Moffitt, and Robert Hoffman, "Waking, Dreaming, and Self-Regulation", in Alan Moffitt, Milton Kramer, and

Robert Hoffman (editors), *The Functions of Dreaming* (Albany: State University of New York Press, 1993), pp. 197-260.

156. Alan Moffitt, "The Creation of Self in Dreaming and Waking", p. 54. Also in Purcell, Moffitt, and Hoffman, "Waking, Dreaming, and Self-Regulation", p. 212.

157. In a private conversation, Dr. Rossi and I have discussed the possibility that stage 4 might be out of place, and should either before the current stage 3 or after the current stage 5. If so, the two most frequent occurring stages—the current stages 3 and 5—would cluster in the middle, as might be expected. In her doctoral dissertation, Dr. Sheila Purcell adapted the Rossi/Moffitt scale to create a 9-stage scale of dream control, as opposed to self-reflectiveness. Analysis of dreams of both frequent and infrequent dream recallers produced a bell-shaped curve under her dream control scale. See Alan Moffitt, "The Creation of Self in Dreaming and Waking", pp. 60-61. Also see Purcell, Moffitt, and Hoffman, "Waking, Dreaming, and Self-Regulation", pp. 216-219, 233-235.

158. See Alan Moffitt, "The Creation of Self in Dreaming and Waking", pp. 56-58.

159. Richard Grossinger, "The Dream Work", in *Dreams are Wiser than Men*, Richard Russo, editor (Berkeley: North Atlantic Books, 1987), p. 191.

160. See John A. Sanford, *Soul Journey: A Jungian Analyst Looks at Reincarnation* (New York: Crossroad, 1991), for a detailed history of the concept of soul. Also see Robin Robertson, *Indra's Net: Alchemy and Chaos Theory as Models for Transformation* (Wheaton, IL: Quest Books, 2009), pp. 27 for a history of the soul in Greek thought.

161. I have previously described this dream more briefly in my book *Beginner's Guide to Jungian Psychology* (York Beach: Nicolas-Hays, 1992), p. 191.

162. Aura Glaser, *A Call to Compassion* (York Beach, ME: Nicolas-Hays, Inc., 2005).

163. M. Esther Harding, *The I and the not-I*, p. 99.

# INDEX

OTHER BOOKS OF INTEREST FROM
# IBIS PRESS
AND
# NICOLAS HAYS

*Beginner's Guide to Jungian Psychology*
Robin Robertson.

In this definitive introduction to the work of C. G. Jung, Dr. Robertson explains how Jung reintroduced Westerners to the world of archetypes—the imagery of the collective unconscious, of mythology, and the symbols in nature. He discusses the structure and dynamics of the psyche, the meaning of dreams, the shadow, the anima/animus, and the mysterious figure of the Self. This practical yet inspiring introduction can make Jung's exciting philosophy/psychology part of your life. "A clear and concise statement of Jung's psychology in a fresh and invigorating way ... unique contributions to Jungian psychology from the point of view of science and the very latest in scientific research."—John A. Sanford, Jungian analyst.
1992 • 240 pp. • 5  x 8 ¼ • ISBN 0-89254-022-2 • Paper, $14.95

*At the End of Time: Prophesy and Revelation, A Spiritual Paradigm*
Robin Robertson.

The Book of Revelation can be interpreted as a saga of changing consciousness. Robertson follows a spiral path around the central issues of our time, drawing from Jung's psychology, neurophysiology, shamanic rituals, and modern mathematics. He reveals how the Book of Revelation symbolically expresses our collective ability to experience the spiritual depths of the universe and helps us take a look at crisis and its affects. Illustrations.
New Edition Revised and Expanded 2011 • 264 pp. • 6  x 9 •
ISBN 0-89254-165-2 • Paper, $18.95

*Mining the Soul: From the Inside Out*
**Robin Robertson.**

Do you think that life happens to you from the outside in? Think again! Robin Robertson says that we are born as complex repositories of memories and behaviors. Yes, we learn some things by rote, but other parts of ourselves—the important things we know in our inner soul before we "know" them in our conscious mind—are waiting to have various "triggers" release them from the silence. Dreams give us a peek at this process. C. G. Jung insisted that we each need to discover our particular myth, the myth of the god or goddess that represents eternal human qualities that still live in us. This book is filled with fact and fiction to show you how you can mine the depths of your psyche in the process of self-development.
2000 • ISBN: 0-89254-055-9 • 288 pp. • 5³/₈"x 8 ³/₈"•Paper • $18.95


*The Way of the Small: Why Less Is More*
**by Michael Gellert**

A practical and spiritual guide to making everyday living sacred. This book explores the principals of a sound, wholesome exisistence for both the individual and society. Addressing the search for finding true happiness, meaning and success, *The Way of the Small* gives us new perspectives based on old wisdom on what makes for a truly lived life. A practical and spiritual guide to fulfillment, it illustrates that happiness is found in "the small"—in ways to celebrate the precious small gifts of ordinary life and experiencing the sacred in all aspects of life. We are reminded that "Less Is More, Simpler Is Better." Michael Gellert is a faculty member of the C.G. Jung Institute of Los Angeles and a certified Jungian analyst in private practice. Psyche illustrates the alchemical process of marrying soul and matter so that life can be lived with more joy, meaning, and a tangible sense of divine love. Alchemy of the Soul takes alchemy from the realm of the esoteric and places it in practical terms of story—terms that anyone can understand, value, and use as a guide to life.
2007 • 192 pp. • 5 x 6 ½ • ISBN: 0892541296 • Paper • $14.95